6008749 | FARR, G. | Wreck & rescue on the Dorset coast

£14.80p 363.123

D1454577

WRECK AND RESCUE ON THE DORSET COAST

THE rugged Isle of Portland, a landfall for mariners since the dawn of navigation, and that wonder of nature the Chesil Beach, not to mention the rugged south face of Purbeck, are all part of the varied Dorset coastal scene. Being so close to the busy shipping lanes up and down the English Channel, and also having a considerable coastal traffic, formerly of traders, but nowadays mainly pleasure craft, it is inevitable that wrecks have occurred from time to time. Some of the older ones, like the East Indiamen *Halsewell* and *Earl of Abergavenny* are classic tales of disaster, but others are relieved by acts of bravery by lifeboatmen and Coastguards. Many of the amazing series of wrecks on the Chesil Beach are described, as also those elsewhere on Portland, on Kimmeridge Ledges, Saint Alban's Head, Lyme Bay and Studland Bay. This history of wreck and rescue on the coast of Dorset is based on detailed research among official records, old newspapers and personal accounts. Like other volumes in the series it tells the story of each of the lifeboat stations, as well as giving check lists both of their rescues and their successive lifeboats.

Wreck and Rescue on the Dorset Coast

THE STORY OF THE DORSET LIFEBOATS

Grahame Farr

D. BRADFORD BARTON LTD
TRURO

ISBN   0 - 85153 - 028 - 1

First published 1971 by
D. BRADFORD BARTON LTD
TRURO BOOKSHOP   TRURO   CORNWALL

© Grahame Farr   1971

Printed by H. E. Warne Ltd   St. Austell

CONTENTS

ILLUSTRATIONS

to
John and Pamela Francis,
in gratitude for their sterling
work on behalf of the
Life-boat Enthusiasts' Society

ABBREVIATIONS

R.N.I.P.L.S.=Royal National Institution for the Preservation of Life from Ship-
wreck (1824-54).
R.N.L.I.   =Royal National Lifeboat Institution (title since 1854).
S.F.M.B.S. =Shipwrecked Fishermen and Mariners' Benevolent Society.

Types of Lifeboat:

B	=Barnett	NC	=North Country
IRB	=Inshore rescue boat		(Greathead)
L	=Liverpool	SR	=Self-righting
(M)	=Motor lifeboat	W	=Watson

NOWADAYS the Dorset coast is largely given over to holiday-makers—
its bays and beaches thick with visitors in the summer and its harbours
full of pleasure craft large and small. Although Weymouth and Poole,
in particular, have been yachting centres for well over a century, it is
doubtful if even twenty years ago anybody could have foretold the
fantastic growth which was to take place in private boat-owning. And
this growth is, of course, of the greatest significance to the subject in
hand—accounting for some 90 per cent of the calls on the Dorset
rescue services.

Seaborne commercial traffic is still to be found at Weymouth and
Poole, and to some extent at Portland, the first named being, of course,
a long established terminal for the Channel Islands traffic. In the last
century there was a great coastal trade in sloops, ketches and schooners
in and out of the harbours, and even on and off the beaches at such
places as Swanage and Lulworth. More sophisticated sailing craft,
brigantines and brigs, sometimes barques, came with timber from the
Baltic and coal from the North-East of England or from Wales. The
outward cargoes were country produce, grains and, predominantly,
stone. Vast quantities of Portland stone and Purbeck marble for
building, as well as the humbler limestone for making lime as a fertiliser,
or for laying roads, were shipped away to leave the scars and pits
which are now part of the rugged Dorset scene. There were also locally
owned fleets, such as the Poole Newfoundlanders, which spent a large
part of their lives trading across the oceans, returning to their home
port for a refit perhaps once a year.

The coastal traffic, as well as deep-sea vessels driven off course, all
too often succumbed to the dangers of the rocky ledges, the beaches and
the races but, somehow, Dorset missed the early distribution of lifeboats which began with the coming of the nineteenth century. Thus,
when the Royal National Institution for the Preservation of Lives from
Shipwreck was founded in 1824 the only means for lifesaving on the
coast of the county were the boats of the Coastguard stations. These
were not fitted as lifeboats with any form of extra buoyancy, or cork

sheathing, but depended on their lightness for quick launching and swift rowing, baling by hand as necessary. Happily the Coastguard, charged with the prevention of smuggling and the discouragement of invasion, had been greatly augmented by experienced naval personnel since the end of the French wars. This highly skilled and dedicated body of men had accomplished some miraculous rescues besides the many minor services which did not reach the press. Subsequently, for many years the Lifeboat Institution, having provided lifeboats and other apparatus designed for the purpose, relied to a great extent upon the Coastguard for its coxswains and crews.

Sir William Hillary, founder of the Institution, had realised the difficulty of building up a national organisation solely from an office in London and had proposed that local associations should be formed. These would enrol the crews, collect funds to reward them and to purchase equipment, with extra financial help and expert advice from the central body when needed. A strong Dorset Branch Association was formed in 1825 under the patronage of the Earls of Digby, Ilchester and Shaftesbury, Lord Rivers and other distinguished gentry. William Morton Pitt, M.P. for Dorchester, apparently undertook the duties of secretary and was indefatigable in his exertions to get practical results. The first step was to place at strategic points the mortars which the government had agreed to release to the National Institution soon after its foundation in the previous year. These were converted to life-saving apparatus by using special shot fitted with resilient thongs of leather and attached to lines in the manner perfected by George Manby. Twelve such apparatus were distributed along the Dorset coast at Lyme, Charmouth, Bridport, Abbotsbury, Fleet, Chesil Cove, Osmington, Lulworth Cove, Warbarrow Bay, Saint Alban's Head, Swanage and North Haven (also called Flag Head).

As regards lifeboats the Dorset Association applied for and were promised two of the 20-feet type built by Plenty of Newbury, but so great was the demand that there were delays in delivery. The boat for Portland arrived early in 1826 and the second, which had been tentatively allocated to Abbotsbury, was sent to Studland Bay on her arrival in the following May or June. A 30-feet lifeboat built by Skelton of Scarborough was also offered, but not taken up, possibly because she was thought too large or probably because she was of an alien type akin to the 'North Country' boats invented by Greathead and never popular except on the east coast. The Portland lifeboat could be launched from either side of Chesil Beach and so afforded some protection for

Weymouth Bay being, in fact, sometimes loosely referred to as the Weymouth boat. Before the two Plenty lifeboats were delivered, however, Lyme Regis had been provided with a shore boat converted for lifesaving on the plan of Captain Spencer of the local Coastguard.

However, the Dorset Branch Association is not mentioned again after the Institution's third annual report, of March 1827, and seems to have become defunct, probably through lack of support in a most difficult period in our kingdom's history. The mortar apparatus, manned by the Coastguard, was superseded by the far more readily transportable rocket apparatus in the 1840's. Swanage, Saint Alban's Head and Kimmeridge were issued with Dennett's rockets in 1842, Abbotsbury in 1844, and Langton received the similar Carte's rockets at about the same time.

By the time of the Duke of Northumberland's *Report*, in 1850, there had been some redistribution of mortar apparatus, but the rockets remained placed as above. Mortars were then at Lyme Cobb (24 lb. calibre), Bridport (two of 6 lb.) Burton (6 lb), and Flag Head (6 lb), the lighter ones being, incidentally, of far more practical use than Lyme's great 'siege gun'. The *Report* further stated that the Burton mortar had been instrumental in saving seven lives at Abbotsbury, and the Bridport unit had saved 'five on one occasion, many others at different times'. The other mortars, the rocket apparatus, and the two lifeboats, both of which were marked 'not worth repair', were not credited with the saving of a single life.

Hot on the heels of his *Report* the 'Sailor Duke' completely rejuvenated the central body and by 1854, when the present title Royal National Life-boat Institution was adopted, there was a rising income, a well-proven pattern of self-righting lifeboat, a diligent inspectorate, and a mood of great enthusiasm among both the shore folk and the public at large. Dorset first felt the benefit of the reforms when a lifeboat was sent to Lyme Regis in 1853, but another twelve years passed before the next lifeboat was sent to Poole, followed by others at Chapman's Pool (usually called the Isle of Purbeck station) in 1866, Kimmeridge in 1868, and Weymouth in 1869. The last station to complete the pattern was Swanage, opened in 1875. Chapman's Pool and Kimmeridge were closed before the end of the century, basically owing to a lack of demand for their services.

The Watson-type sailing lifeboat came to Poole in 1897 and Weymouth in 1903, but the really great advance was the motor lifeboat. Dorset's first was sent to Weymouth in 1924, followed by Swanage in

1928 and Poole in 1939. The Lyme Regis station was closed in 1932 as demand in that area had dropped. After the Second World War, however, the increase in pleasure boating led to a change in the situation and Lyme was reopened in 1967 with an Inshore Rescue Boat. Poole, with its large harbour so popular with week-end yachtsmen, had been given one of these useful light rescue craft in 1964 on an experimental basis, and the station was permanently established in the following year. Both stations have taken a hand in testing new forms of small, fast rescue craft which have proved a tremendous boon in dealing with estuarial and coastal casualties.

As a further means of dealing with inshore incidents the R.N.L.I., in conjunction with the Coastguard, instituted an Inshore Rescue Scheme in 1962 in which owners of suitable craft were invited to participate. Their names were to be noted by the Coastguard and in suitable conditions of weather they could be called out to deal with small craft casualties, receiving payment similar to that of lifeboatmen, and expenses. At first the scheme centred upon the Isle of Wight district, reaching westwards as far as Swanage, but in 1964 it was extended to cover the whole coastline of England and Wales.

As far as air rescue services are concerned, Royal Navy 'Whirlwind' and 'Wessex' helicopters are stationed at Portland for daylight use. The regional Search and Rescue Headquarters, which is there to co-ordinate the efforts of long range aircraft and all manner of shipping in dealing with distress calls farther afield, is at Plymouth.

The Coastguard for practically the whole county comes under the Wyke Division of the Southern District, the short length of coast eastwards from Poole Harbour entrance to the county boundary, and beyond, being in the Needles Division of the South-Eastern District. Constant watches are kept at Divisional Headquarters at Wyke, at Portland Bill, and at Saint Alban's Head. Watches, occasional in fine weather but constant in bad, are kept at Grove Point (Portland), Swanage and Southbourne, Hants. There are posts manned by Coastguard Auxiliaries in bad weather at West Bay, Abbotsbury, Lulworth and Studland. Rocket apparatus is kept at Fortuneswell (Portland), Saint Alban's Head, Swanage and Southbourne, and various types of pistol rescue apparatus at West Bay, Abbotsbury, Langton, Fleet, Wyke, Portland Bill, Lulworth and Mudeford (Hants).

So far Dorset boatyards have not built lifeboats, although surveys and repairs are often carried out at a yard at Hamworthy. Only one Dorset man submitted a plan for the Northumberland Prize competition in 1850, he being C. Besant of Weymouth, whose ideas for a 24-feet ten-oared boat costing only £30 did not appeal sufficiently to the judges to obtain a significant marking. Weymouth had also, in earlier years, played a part in the development of the tubular lifeboat, a catamaran type which became popular in North Wales and the Mersey estuary. Henry Richardson, of Bala in Wales, superintended the building of four boats of this type in different sizes at Weymouth during 1830-1, and took them to his home lake for trials. He submitted plans to the Northumberland Prize Committee and afterwards, feeling his design had not received the attention it merited, built a prototype tubular lifeboat in which he made a long coastal passage.

Right from the early years of the nineteenth century lifeboat inventors have been busy and many peculiar creations have been publicised briefly. Among those which reached the stage of building and testing a prototype was one that was tried at Weymouth in 1805. Probably the disastrous loss of the *Earl of Abergavenny* with more than three hundred lives on the Shingles Bank, off Portland, led to this invention. She was described in the *Annual Register* under the date August 29th 1805, and in several other contemporary publications, but unfortunately no later information has come to light.

'The new invented life-boat, with which experiments have been making at Weymouth for some time past, is considered to be well calculated to answer the purpose for which it is intended. When sailing from Teignmouth to Weymouth, her stern ports were all the time open. She is buoyed up by eight cases, four on each side, water tight, and independent of each other. When men are saved from a wreck and landed, the boat may return, and some tons of goods may be put in the cases if the sea will admit of its being taken out of the wrecked vessel. In a storm the boat is dismantled, and rowed by fourteen men, who are fastened to their seats. As the sea breaks into the boat, it immediately runs out at her stern-ports. It is impossible to sink her. She has fourteen life-lines, the ends of which float with cork, by which men that are washed off the wreck may hold, before they can be taken into the boat. She brings before the wind, or nearly so, upwards of one hundred men at a time from the wreck. She is as manageable with sails as any boat of her size. The rudder is on a new principle, she has fourteen grapnels for a wreck, a room ten feet wide, water tight, with copper ventilators. The whole of her construction is entirely new.'

Indeed a most intriguing craft, but the claim that she could hold more than a hundred men in addition to her crew, suggests something larger than we might expect. 'Dismantled' should presumably be 'dismasted', meaning that the mast would be unstepped and stowed.

As with earlier volumes in this series the publications and records of the R.N.L.I., particularly the *Annual Reports*, the quarterly journal *The Life-boat*, and the *War History* have provided the basis for the station histories. The background and the stories of wrecks before the lifeboat era have been culled from many sources—local newspapers, Parliamentary Papers, and the like. In the cause of accuracy ships' names and other details have been checked wherever possible by specialised publications such as the *Mercantile Navy List*, *Lloyd's Register of Shipping*, *Lloyd's Yacht Register*, and *Lloyd's List*. Needless to say the author would welcome corrections for the benefit of future editions, and also further photographs of wrecks and rescue work. Many interesting questions have been answered by correspondence with readers of earlier volumes. However, it must be borne in mind that it is impossible to describe every wreck in the area concerned, and many tales of disaster and heroism must necessarily go untold. The local newspapers did, of course, publish topical reports of lifeboat activities, although there is a dearth of reports before the 1850's and, in general, the Dorset literature took little notice of wreck and rescue. In recent years four local histories were written and published in booklet form for sale at the stations:—

One Hundred Years of Life-saving at Sea; the story of the lifeboat service at Poole, 1865-1965, (published 1965) by Harry C. Matthews and others.

Rescue, the Story of the Swanage Lifeboats from 1875 by E. L. Millward (1953, reprinted 1964).

A Hundred Years of Lifesaving, 1869-1969: a History of the Weymouth Life-boat Station, (published 1969) by David J. Hancox.

Deep End, The Story of the Lyme Regis Lifeboats, (1969) by David Cozens.

For the broader history of the lifeboat service one can do no better than read Major A. J. Dawson's *Britain's Life-boats*, published in 1924 to mark the centenary of the R.N.L.I. It can be brought closer to date with Patrick Howarth's *The Life-boat Story* (Routledge and Kegan Paul, 1957), and the late J. R. Barnett's *Modern Motor Life-boats* (Blackie, 1950). The R.N.L.I. annual booklet *The Story of the Life-boats* can be recommended for topical reading on the service.

Membership of the Life-boat Enthusiasts' Society, which is under the patronage of the R.N.L.I., is useful to those who are more deeply interested in lifeboat history and design. The honorary secretary is John G. Francis, 20a Transmere Road, Pett's Wood, Orpington, Kent.

Grateful acknowledgement is made for help received from the following individuals and institutions: D. Bradford Barton, my publisher; Patrick Howarth, S. E. Bartholomew and Christopher Elliott of the R.N.L.I.; Eric Latcham, of Weymouth; Miss Frances Reynolds of the Bridport Museum and Art Gallery, and Miss Valerie Wood, of Poole. For photographs I am indebted to several of the above and also to John Behenna, of Galmpton; Mr. Haysom of Swanage, and his son John; Mr. Gerald Silverlock of Lyme Regis; and Mr. and Mrs. Marshall, of Kimmeridge.

GRAHAME FARR

May 1970   Portishead

1

LYME REGIS

THE COBB, the ancient harbour of Lyme Regis, is thought to date from the thirteenth century. Today its massive arms protect pleasure craft, but for several centuries it accommodated commerce—the brigs, schooners and smacks which brought in all manner of goods and went away with the local products—mainly serges, salt and stone. Indeed until 1880 Lyme was a fully fledged Customs Port, a fact which speaks for its former maritime importance.

The old harbour was not sufficiently spacious for a harbour of refuge, but in westerly and southerly gales vessels were often embayed in Lyme Bay and the *Pilot's Handbook* recommended masters faced with an emergency to 'run in and save life if not property'. Vessels which could not reach Lyme were usually washed under the cliffs to the east. Bridport harbour, about seven miles in that direction, is entered through a north-easterly channel and is little help in a crisis. As the *Pilot* warned: in south-westerly gales the sea breaks so heavily at the entrance that the harbour is unapproachable.

Some early wrecks are on record. In August 1789 the brig *Endeavour* left the beach at Sidmouth, bound light for Newcastle to fetch another cargo of coal, but was thrown ashore in a storm near Bridport—'the crew were with difficulty saved'. On February 21st 1812, two vessels, the schooner *Fox*, bound from London for Exeter, and the smack *Henrietta*, London for Bridport, were driven ashore nearby and totally wrecked, their crews also being saved. On another stormy night, January 19th 1817, the *Trois Amis*, of Bordeaux, was lost near Bridport with only one man saved, while at about the same time another French vessel, an unidentified wine-laden chasse-marree was lost with all hands at Charmouth beach.

It was after the hurricane which struck the Dorset coast on November 23rd 1824 that serious representations were made by the merchants and gentry of the district for the provision of life-saving equipment. On that occasion, when the storm was at its height a tidal wave completely submerged the Cobb. Every vessel within was blown or washed out. Some made an offing and rode out the storm, but among others the London trader *Unity* was driven ashore between Lyme and Charmouth. It was the occasion of an epic rescue and a spirited painting of the scene, by Carter Galpin, is to be seen in the local museum. Captain C. C. Bennett, R.N., with two helpers, William Porter and John Freeman, saved the crew of four after a terrific struggle in the surf. An extract from a memorial which was sent to the Admiralty will give a few details of the courageous rescue:—'Captain Bennett observed different vessels break from their moorings and drift rapidly towards the cliffs at Charmouth. He immediately provided himself with rope and lines out of his pleasure yacht and proceeded along the shore. When opposite a vessel that was stranded he got down on a projecting part of the cliff and was followed by others, particularly by Thomas Porter, a pilot, who, being secured by a rope, went on board the vessel and succeeded in rescuing the master, who was safely hauled on shore. Whilst this was doing one of the crew of the vessel fell from the rigging into the sea, entirely exhausted. Captain Bennett immediately slipped down the cliff with a rope round his body, and at the risk of his own life rushed into the sea and after some search succeeded in recovering the body, and with assistance dragged him safe on shore.' John Freeman also joined them and the remaining two men, a seaman and a boy, had to be cut from the rigging and dragged ashore being so much bruised and exhausted from clinging for dear life while the wreck was constantly covered by seas and rolling violently.

It was afterwards found that William Porter and not Thomas, was the rescuer of Captain Pearce and he with John Freeman was awarded the silver medal of the recently formed Royal National Institution for the Preservation of Life from Shipwreck. Captain C. C. Bennett, R.N., received the gold medal.

While Lyme set about repairing its battered sea front—the Cobb had to be substantially rebuilt at the precise cost of £17,337.0s.9¼d., a large sum of money in those days—the government agreed to supply mortars adapted as life-saving apparatus on the Manby plan. Bridport and Charmouth had light outfits of 6 lb. calibre, the former of which saved life on many occasions. Unfortunately Lyme was given a massive 24 lb. mortar which could, of course, fire its line a greater distance, but was so heavy as to be hardly transportable beyond the paved area of the harbour.

As regards a lifeboat, William Morton Pitt, the M.P. for Dorchester, who was actively assisting the Dorset Branch Association to become effective, wrote to the parent Institution on August 10th 1825, saying that Captain R. Spencer, R.N., of Lyme Regis, had devised a plan to convert ordinary boats for life-saving. He was being asked to convert a local boat and report on the result. Spencer duly reported by letter on October 17th saying that he had fitted airtight cases under the thwarts and lashed others outside each gunnel. Although the gallant Captain did not mention it, he had to carry out his trials personally since the local pilots refused to assist. The Dorset Committee considered the boat had acquitted herself admirably and suggested that the plan of conversion should be published so that authorities at other ports could adopt the same method. After due deliberation the central committee suggested that further air-boxes should be placed under the fore sheets and after sheets for additional buoyancy, but that cork should be laid along the gunnels instead of air-boxes as being a more durable fender when going alongside a wreck. They also suggested that 14 oz. copper was the most suitable material for making the airtight boxes.

Unfortunately we have found no further reference to the Spencer lifeboat or information of any rescues she might have attempted or accomplished. In the next two decades there were just two instances where the Institution made rewards for rescues at Lyme, but in neither case is there mention of a lifeboat. The first occasion was in December 1836, when Coastguard John Keogh led a crew to save four of the five men on board the schooner *William and Ann*, but unfortunately he lost his own life in a further attempt to save the vessel's stores. Then, in October 1839, pilot Thomas Rogers was rewarded for saving a Coastguard by means of a boat. On the Christmas Day following this last rescue the coastline west of Lyme was the scene of a great landslip when tens of thousands of tons of mud and stones thundered down to the beach. Often through the centuries parts of the coast of Lyme Bay have been altered in this way.

In October 1851, Captain Willoughby, R.N., the Inspecting Commander of Coastguards for the district, wrote to the Institution stating the case for a lifeboat. They deliberated at some length and in June of the following year asked Willoughby what had happened to the Spencer lifeboat. He replied that when tried the boat capsized, nearly drowning one man. Apparently she had lain neglected until the Coastguards dismantled her and sold the copper cases, her most valuable parts, for 'old stores'. Four months later, after study of wreck reports, the Institution agreed to supply a Peake-type self-righter if two-thirds of the cost could be subscribed locally. This was the usual manner in which the slender funds of the Institution were made to help many localities. However, before the boat arrived there was a spectacular wreck on the rocks close to the Cobb.

The barque *Heroine*, of London, outward bound with emigrants for Port Philip, Australia, came ashore in a hurricane on Boxing Day and soon foundered. After she had struck the rocks the crew, by a combination of good fortune and seamanship, were able to launch their long-boat and another small boat and the whole complement of 44, including passengers, got ashore safely. They were helped by a boat from the revenue cruiser *Frances*, which went out to direct them to the harbour entrance. Unfortunately this small craft was upset in the surf and four of the five brave men were drowned. They comprised three of the *Frances*' crew and the mate of the schooner *Honiton Packet*. A fund was raised for the widows and orphans, and the Institution, giving a sum of money to the fund, also awarded its silver medal to the one survivor, William Bridle, master of the cutter *Primrose*. In the same great storm there were two other wrecks in the vicinity and the Coast-guards, the crew of the revenue cruiser, and many local seamen were actively engaged in rescue work.

The lifeboat arrived in September 1853. She was a light 27-feet eight-oared self-righter and was housed in a shed under a sail loft rented at £3 per annum. Not many months elapsed before she was called out on service. On January 7th, while a gale from the S.S.W. was raging, a brigantine was seen about five miles off with a flag of distress in her rigging. With eight Coastguards and four seamen—two extra hands to double-bank the midship oars—the lifeboat was rowed out through the surf almost into the teeth of the gale. After a hard pull they arrived alongside the distressed vessel and found her to be the *Jeune Rose*, of Bayonne, with her hold almost full of water, her crew exhausted with pumping and weak with lack of sleep and food. Seven lifeboatmen went on board the rolling craft and quickly repaired the broken rigging, bent new sails and managed to pump out some of the water. The storm continued unabated, however, and as they were just beginning their first tack back towards Lyme, a heavy squall thundered down and sent the brigantine over on her beam ends, her heavy deck load of rosin in barrels contributing to her unsteadiness. The situation was desperate for in rolling over her main sail and boom caught the lifeboat towing on her lee side. At the same time several barrels broke loose and were tumbled over the rails, with the result that the lifeboat was herself forced over and capsized. Five men were in her at the time and of these two jumped clear, but the Coxswain and two others were trapped underneath. After some twenty minutes, which must have seemed a lifetime to the men trapped in the air-pocket under the boat, the brigantine partly righted herself and the Coxswain struggled clear. He handed his knife to another man who slashed the sails and rigging, so allowing the lifeboat to right, but it was found that Coastguard John Martin had drowned. With remarkably little damage to herself, the lifeboat was then righted, both crews were taken on board, and they sailed back to the Cobb under an improvised rig. For leading this arduous operation Coxswain Boxhall was awarded a silver medal by the Emperor of the French.

In August 1856, there was a daring shoreboat rescue off Lyme when William Calloway, alone in his boat, saved two men from another boat which had capsized. He plunged into the sea in an attempt to save a third drowning man, but in spite of all his efforts he was defeated by the currents. Calloway received the Institution's silver medal.

The lifeboat's second service came on October 7th 1857, when she was launched with an augmented crew of twelve men and gave help to five vessels anchored in the bay when a sudden gale threatened to break them adrift.

In 1860 a new 30-feet lifeboat with ten oars was sent to the station, built by Semmens of Penzance on the Peake self-righting plan. Soon after her arrival she was thoroughly tested in a long and difficult rescue. On the night of August 18th, a heavy gale was raging from the W.S.W., when news was received of a vessel anchored dangerously close to the lee shore at the western end of the Chesil Beach, about fifteen miles east of Lyme. The lifeboat was launched at 4 a.m. on the 19th, to take advantage of the tide, and after four and a half hours sailing, during which the waves continually broke over her, she came upon the locally-owned brig *Ceres*. The *Ceres* was disabled by the loss of her foretopmast and some sails, and her safety depended solely upon her anchors at which she was rolling and tugging heavily. Some lifeboatmen went on board to help repair the broken spars and about noon, the weather moderating, they were able to weigh one anchor, slip the second, and make for Bridport harbour, which they reached at seven in the evening.

Some three months later, on the evening of November 14th, the boat was again launched into a whole gale and complete darkness to the help of the coal-laden smack *Elizabeth Ann*, which was driven on to the rocks behind the harbour wall. In a most dangerous situation the lifeboat was eased between the rocks, the forward oarsmen fending off and the rest intently watching the coxswain as he gave orders for the necessary delicate manoeuvring. The smack's crew of three, all Lyme men, were snatched from their partly submerged vessel in the nick of time. A further service in 1863 in which the schooner *Vulcan* was saved from being dashed on to the rocks in a strong gale, proved to be the last service of this lifeboat.

There have been only four or five cases where women have been awarded the R.N.L.I. medal, the best known being the Northumbrian heroine Grace Darling. In August 1864, a young lady 'sojourning at Lyme Regis' joined the select band. She was rowing in the shelter of the Cobb with a lady friend when her attention was drawn to a commotion on the outer breakwater where two small boys had fallen into the sea. At that exposed point the waves were beating heavily on the rocks, but Miss Alice le Geyt without hesitation turned her small boat seawards. With the waves threatening to swamp them at any moment the intrepid girl used an oar to steady and manoeuvre the boat while she helped her companion to haul the two cold and frightened children aboard. In this a high degree of skill was needed and the difficulties must have been increased by the voluminous female dress of the period.

In 1866 the Semmens lifeboat was found to have symptoms of decay and was condemned. The opportunity was taken to reorganise the station with a larger lifeboat, named *William Woodcock*, given by an anonymous Manchester lady. The original fish-cellar house having been found inconvenient for the 27-feet and 30-feet boats, was quite impracticable for this 33-feet craft. Thus it was necessary to build a new house on the nearest available land, fifty yards or so to the west of the Cobb.

The *William Woodcock* arrived on station in December 1866, but in attempting to launch her from the west beach it was found impossible to get her to sea during a heavy south-westerly gale on January 8th following. No less than five vessels, mostly locally owned, the *Lyn*, *Spec, Ann and Emily, Maria* and *Vulcan*, were thrown on to the beaches on either side of the Cobb. Some were without crews, having been driven from their moorings, but Lieutenant W. H. Elton, the Coastguard commander, with a crew of five made up of two of his men, two master mariners and a seaman, launched the station galley to investigate. After an anxious time in their light craft they saved three men, two from the *Vulcan* and one from the *Maria*. Elton was afterwards awarded the R.N.L.I. silver medal and his volunteer crew rewarded. Commander

W. T. Newenham, late Chief Officer of the Lyme Coastguard, in a letter to *The Times*, described the occasion 'as one of the most fearful storms experienced'. He thought if the lifeboat had been available to place crews on two of the vessels they might have been saved. He also said it was proved impossible to launch the lifeboat near her present house, but did not say why she was not taken to the harbour for launching as her predecessors were. Possibly the roadway was obstructed by boats drawn up out of reach of the waves.

A year later, on January 17th 1868, the lifeboat was vindicated when she was launched into a strong south-westerly gale to help the schooner *Kate*, of Ipswich, dragging her anchors shorewards from a position off the Cobb. The seas were very heavy and the schooner was surrounded by broken water, but with lifeboatmen put on board they set a small steering sail, raised one anchor and buoyed the other. She was then manoeuvred to the harbour entrance and with many willing hands manning the massive warp which was always kept ready at the pier head for such emergencies, she was 'tracked' to a safe berth.

On November 26th 1872, a ship's boat full of men was seen off Lyme being blown rapidly towards the breakers which in the existing gale conditions stretched a considerable distance from the shore. The lifeboat was got away in record time and was able to intercept the boat just before she reached the surf-line. The fourteen men who were saved had escaped from the Shields barque *Cassibelaunus* which had foundered many miles away off Start Point in the early morning.

It was eighteen years before a further rescue could be added to the station record, but meanwhile there was a most unusual and tragic accident. On December 10th 1881, the government balloon *Saladin* left Bath on a demonstration flight. Captain Templar, Royal Engineers, was in charge, and one of his two passengers was a Westcountry Member of Parliament. In a fresh breeze the balloon was blown across the counties of Somerset and Dorset and when it became obvious they would be blown out to sea, Captain Templar allowed some gas to escape so that they came to earth near Bridport. They came down with considerable impact, the Captain and one of his passengers being more or less thrown out of the gondola. Unfortunately, Walter Powell, the M.P., was not swift enough in getting out, and the balloon, relieved suddenly of two-thirds of its freight, sprang into the air again carrying the unfortunate man out over the sea. He was never seen again although the Lyme Regis lifeboat and several other craft searched all night.

In 1884 a new lifeboat house was built nearer the harbour in a position more convenient for launching. The new establishment cost more than £500 and the old house was given to the vendor of the plot of land in part exchange. Both houses stand to this day, the newer one being used as a cafe, and the older, now usually surrounded by parked cars, caters for other essential needs.

The last service of the *Woodcock* came on November 7th 1890, when she went off to the Brixham fishing ketch *Rescue* which was seen to come to an anchor and hoist a signal of distress some four miles off. She was found to have lost spars and sails so the lifeboat's spare mainsail was taken aboard by some lifeboatmen, who also helped to bend and set it. After this the ketch and her crew of four were able to reach the shelter of the Cobb.

In July 1891, one of the latest pattern 34-feet water-ballast self-righting lifeboats was sent to Lyme. She was one of a number provided and endowed by Charles Carr Ashley, of Kingston-on-Thames and Mentone and was named *Susan Ashley* after the donor's mother, who had lately died. By the 1890's, however, local commercial traffic had declined drastically. One result was that although the *Susan Ashley* had eight service launches, only one was classed as a 'service'—that being on the night of November 27-28th 1910, when she helped the German barque *Fürst Bismarck*. This vessel had been driven towards the lee shore in a strong south-easterly gale, and was pulled up by her anchors in an extremely dangerous position. At about 9.40 p.m. on the 27th she hoisted a signal of distress and the lifeboatmen found her master fully expecting she would drive ashore. He asked them to stand by and this was done through the night. By the morning the wind had dropped considerably and the lifeboatmen helped to weigh the anchors so that the barque could continue her voyage from Bremen to Trinidad.

Of the *Susan Ashley*'s seven unsuccessful launches, four were to casualties on the western section of the Chesil Beach and, with a sailing and pulling lifeboat, the distance made such a venture something of a forlorn hope. In the cases of the Greek steamer *Lamyron* (night of 13th-14th August 1907); Norwegian steamer *Noreg* (30th November 1914), and the French ketch *Reine* (5th December 1914), tugs from Weymouth reached the scene first. When the steamer *Dorothea*, of Rotterdam, went ashore at Langton during the night of 14th-15th February 1914, the crew were able to walk ashore at low water. The final service launch of this lifeboat was on 11th December 1914, when the Weymouth fishing vessel *Emma and John* was driving ashore under the cliffs a little way to the east. In the southerly gale huge seas were sweeping across the entrance to the Cobb and during three attempts to get to sea the lifeboat was damaged against the harbour wall. Repairs and further efforts were made until it was reported that the crew of the distressed vessel had got ashore.

In 1915 the *Susan Ashley* was condemned and sold locally for the reported sum of £8.10s. At a later date, when she had been a trip-boat named *Blue Bird*, somebody proposed to cross the Atlantic in her, but she got no farther than Ireland. Her replacement in 1915 was a new 35-feet lifeboat of the same class, one of the last dozen sailing lifeboats to be built. She came from a yard at East Cowes and was named *Thomas Masterman Hardy*. Her first service, on March 18th 1918, was to save five of the crew of the large steamer *Baygitano* which had been torpedoed by a German submarine a mile and a half to the south-west. Two or three men were killed in the explosion, but thanks to calm weather all the rest got away either in the lifeboat or the ship's boats.

Of the eleven launches of the *Hardy*, three were recorded as successful, the last two being stand-by cases. In 1920 she assisted and arranged a tug for the motor fishing ketch *Sheila Margaret*, of Southampton, which had broken down near the cliffs to the east of Lyme, and in 1922

she helped a vessel with the unusual rig of a five-masted schooner. During the war a number of such multi-masted wooden schooners with auxiliary motors were built in Canada. The idea behind the scheme was to conserve steel plate and fuel, the cargoes they were to carry, mainly of timber, being not of a really urgent nature. The five-master *Jessie Norcross*, of Vancouver, was carrying a cargo of coal and a large crew of 25 when she found herself embayed off Abbotsbury in a gale from the W.S.W. Her motor was giving trouble and most of her sails had been blown away or torn. When one anchor cable parted the danger of being thrown on to the Chesil Beach was imminent and the lifeboat was called. Then, after they had stood by all night, the wind moderated and the lifeboat returned to Lyme, where the Coxswain arranged by telegraph for a tug to go to the schooner. She was then towed to Portland naval base for which her cargo had been destined.

When ten years had passed since the last service the closure of the station was officially discussed. The *Hardy* had been launched on January 12th 1930, to a storm-battered ketch seen drifting across Lyme Bay which proved to be the *Reine des Cieux*, of Paimpol, from which the Torbay lifeboat had already saved the crew of three.

9   0   1   2   3

C   H   A   N   N   E   L

Nothing could be done to save the derelict and she was eventually driven ashore at Eype, just west of Bridport, where she quickly went to pieces. However, this genuine service call did not avert the decision to close being made at a committee meeting on October 13th 1932. A motor lifeboat was being built for the neighbouring station at Exmouth and this was considered capable of meeting the needs of the northern parts of Lyme Bay, while the powerful motor lifeboats at Torbay to the west and Weymouth to the east could cover the Channel shipping lanes from which most casualties originated.

The closure was basically the result of the changing pattern of coastal shipping, and later it was the coming of another change—the boom in pleasure boating—that led to the reopening of the station in 1967. One of the fast inflatable inshore rescue boats was then brought to the Cobb and a new house built by voluntary labour right on the shore of the harbour. There was a formal inauguration on June 10th, but in fact the I.R.B. had already made two services, saving two from the yacht *Wren* on June 7th, and landing four from the speedboat *Black Panther* on the following day. All told the I.R.B. had a most successful first season with seven services and fourteen lives saved.

One rescue of five from the capsized cabin cruiser *Lilian*, on June 25th, resulted in the award of the formal Thanks inscribed on vellum to her crew, Robert Jefford and Lionel Fisher. It was at about four on this Sunday afternoon that the yacht capsized in choppy seas to the east of Lyme Regis. A phone call was put through to the honorary secretary and taken by his wife who at once sounded the klaxon alarm at the boathouse. The I.R.B. was away in three minutes and went at full speed to the casualty. They found the cruiser low in the water and almost keel-upwards. A rowing boat had put off from the shore and was rescuing one man. A woman was clinging to the yacht's keel, two boys were hanging on to her bows and another man was in the water nearby. The man in the water was first pulled in by means of the inflated ring and line, then the woman and two boys were taken aboard. All were in a dazed condition. Thinking they had saved all they were about to return to the Cobb when the man said an elderly lady was in the cabin, probably trapped under water, having been there some time. The I.R.B. crew at once tried to right the cruiser and managed to turn her on her side. One held her as still as possible and the other then had to break open the door by pulling it from its hinges. He was groping in the cabin when the inrush of water washed the woman out. She was dragged on board the I.R.B. and mouth to mouth resuscitation was applied while they returned to the Cobb at full speed. A doctor was awaiting them and gave further treatment. All five survived.

In 1968 an experimental I.R.B. designed and built by the pupils of Atlantic College, at St. Donats, in South Wales, was on trial at Lyme. Slightly larger than the standard I.R.B., the *X.5* has a rigid 'V'-shaped bottom, a helmsman's seat—which avoids the tiring kneeling position, wheel steering plus a console with the instruments and controls close to hand.

Towards the end of the 1968 season the experimental I.R.B. was returned to Atlantic College and it was the standard I.R.B. which was involved in the unfortunate fatality of January 17th 1969. The catamaran *Karuna*, owned by an American, had been abandoned at sea after a collision with a tanker in the previous October but later found and towed to Lyme Regis pending the settlement of a claim for salvage. During a gale on January 17th the catamaran was torn from her moorings and drifted eastward. Three men of the I.R.B. crews were given permission to go out and attempt to tow the yacht back to harbour, but in heavy seas close under the cliffs the I.R.B. was capsized, and all were thrown into the sea. Two reached shore safely but Robert Jefford was drowned.

Early in 1969, while retaining the standard inflatable I.R.B., the Lyme Regis station received for evaluation trials the second of a new class of fibreglass rescue launches based on the Dell Quay Dory type of hull. These are 17 ft. 1½ in. long and of 7 ft. beam with a draught of 18 in. with the motors in use, or only 8 in. with motors raised. They are powered by twin Penta outboard motors each of 36 h.p. which give a maximum speed of 25 knots and with normal fuel tanks can cover 110 miles. Soon after the new rescue boat arrived on the station the family of the late Reverend G. F. Eyre, of Lyme Regis, kindly gave her cost to the R.N.L.I. and asked that she should be named *Bob Abbott* in memory of Coxswain Robert West Abbott who was in charge on the station from 1903 to 1925. As will be seen by the service lists both the rescue boats have made a number of useful services.

It is surprising how rarely the lifeboats to the west and east were called upon to come as far as Bridport but, as noted in the introduction, the mortar and rocket apparatus was able to deal with a number of casualties in this vicinity. The port flourished for about fifty years, between 1830 and 1880, but trade diminished subsequently although the spacious basin has accommodated trading vessels on many occasions since then.

A number of wrecks are recorded for this area, such as the brigantine *Black Diamond*, of Ardrossan, with a cargo of oats in 1865, and on January 24th 1868, the barque *Marie Leocadie*, probably the largest vessel owned in the port, which foundered between the piers effectively blocking the entrance. On January 22nd 1869, the Exeter brigantine *Demetrius* was driven on to the East Beach, her crew being saved, but on December 30th in the same year the *Louis et Eugenie*, of Nantes, blown seriously off course when on passage with wheat between two French ports, was wrecked to the west of the harbour and two of her crew drowned. On October 26th 1870, the *Kennett*, of Rye, inward bound with oats from Ireland, stranded on the same beach, and on August 27th 1887, the cutter *King George*, bound from Lyme for Bridport with limestone, struck the nearby Black Rocks. Then there were three wrecks spread over a quarter century, all showing the dangers of leaving the harbour when there was insufficient wind to take a sailing vessel past the incoming breakers. On January 18th 1895, it was the London ketch *Olive*, homeward bound with a cargo of Bridport grit, and on March 12th 1903, it was the Runcorn schooner *Albion*, with the same cargo. Twenty years later, on May 13th 1923, the master of the Swedish ketch *Alioth*, impatient to leave after discharging his timber cargo, sailed out against the advice of the pilots and was washed on to the East Beach. The Coastguard established a rope communication by which means the crew came ashore.

BOAT RECORD, LYME REGIS

Years on Station	Length, Breadth, Oars/Crew	Type, Weight, Cost	Year built, (Off. No.), Builder	Boat's Name, Donor, Authority
1825-?		*	c. 1825	(Name, if any, unknown) Local subscription Dorset Branch Association
1853-1860	27' 7' 6" 8/9	Peake 2t £137	1853 Forrestt, Limehouse	(No name) R.N.I.P.L.S. and local subscriptions R.N.I.P.L.S. / 1854-R.N.L.I.
1860-1866	30' 8' 10/12	Peake 2t5 £150	1853 Semmens, Penzance	(No name) R.N.L.I. R.N.L.I.
1866-1891	33" 8' 10/13	SR 2t5 £278	1866 (214) Forrestt, Limehouse	*William Woodcock* 'H.W.'(a lady of Manchester) R.N.L.I.

* A local boat adapted for life-saving on the plan of Captain R. Spencer, R.N.; see text.

1891-	34'	SR	1891 (322)	*Susan Ashley*
1915	8'	3t17	Forrestt,	Chas. Carr Ashley, Mentone
	10/13	£420	Limehouse	R.N.L.I.
1915-	35'	SR	1915 (650)	*Thomas Masterman Hardy*
1932	8' 6"	3t18	Saunders,	Mrs. John Thynne, London
	10/13	£1623	E. Cowes	R.N.L.I.

Inshore Rescue Boats

1967-	15' 6"	standard I.R.B.
1968	17' 6"	special experimental model *X.*5
1969-	17'	fast rescue launch *Bob Abbott* (17-002)

SERVICE RECORD, LYME REGIS

Lifeboat of 1853

| 1854 | Jan. | 7 | Brigantine *La Jeune Rose*, of Bayonne, saved | 5 |
| 1857 | Oct. | 7 | Five vessels anchored off the shore, gave help | |

Lifeboat of 1860

1860	Aug.	19	Schooner *Ceres*, of Lyme, stood by and assisted to safety at Bridport	
	Nov.	14	Smack *Elizabeth Ann*, of Lyme, saved	3
1863	May	19	Schooner *Vulcan*, of Lyme, saved vessel	

William Woodcock Lifeboat

1868	Jan.	17	Smack *Kate*, of Ipswich, assisted to save smack and	4
1872	Nov.	26	Boat of barque *Cassibelaunus*, of North Shields, saved	14
1890	Nov.	7	Ketch *Rescue*, of Brixham, saved vessel and	4

Susan Ashley Lifeboat

| 1910 | Nov. 27-28 | Barque *Fürst Bismarck*, of Brake (West Germany), stood by and gave help | |

Thomas Masterman Hardy Lifeboat

1918	Mar.	18	Steamship *Baygitano*, of Cardiff, saved	5
1920	Oct.	21	Motor ketch *Sheila Margaret*, of Southampton, stood by and assisted to save vessel	
1922	Apr.	15	Auxiliary five-masted schooner *Jessie Norcross*, of Vancouver (British Columbia), stood by	

(Station closed 1932-1967)

Inshore Rescue Boat

1967	June	7	Yacht *Wren*, saved	2
		8	Speed-boat *Black Panther*, gave help and landed 4	
		25	Cabin cruiser *Lilian*, saved	5
	July	8	Canoe, saved	1
	Aug.	2	Motor dinghy, saved dinghy and	2
		5	People cut off by the tide at Gun Cliff, saved	4
		16	Yacht *Shelandre*, escorted yacht	
1968	July	15	*Hunter* aircraft, gave help	
	July	27	Motor cruiser in tow, escorted boats	
1969	April	7	Dinghy, gave help and escorted dinghy	
	May	28	Sailing dinghy *Blue Chip*, gave help	
	Oct.	9	Person cut off by tide, saved	1
1970	April	12	Motor fishing vessel *Lulworth Fisher*, of Weymouth, saved boat and	3

Rescue Launch *Bob Abbott* (17-002)

1969	April	20	Cabin cruiser *Presgold*, saved cruiser and	2
	July	20	Cabin cruiser *Cemar*, gave help	
	Aug.	8	Yacht *Elizian*, gave help	
	Aug.	25	'Mirror' class sailing dinghy, saved dinghy and	1
	Sept.	3	Dinghy, saved dinghy and	1

2

PORTLAND AND WEYMOUTH

THE BILL OF PORTLAND, a massive limestone wedge three-and-a-half miles by one-and-a-quarter, and nearly 500 feet high at its northern end, has served as a landfall for vessels passing up and down the English Channel since the dawn of navigation. But like all popular landfalls it has also been the scene of many a disastrous wreck. Vessels approaching from the west, in particular, may have made a slight error in calculating their course across Lyme Bay, failing to allow for the currents, or in the case of sailing vessels, for a slight southerly change in the direction of wind. They have thus approached the sheer cliffs of the 'island' or gone farther north into West Bay where they would have to anchor off Chesil Beach—not a bad anchorage in places, but in westerly or southerly weather where ground tackle must stand the strain or it will prove a last resting place.

The Chesil Beach is famous as a phenomenon of nature. Billions of pebbles have been thrown up in an arc of eighteen miles stretching north and west between Portland and Burton Cliffs. The belt averages 200 yards in breadth and is fifty to sixty feet above normal sea level. The current is northward so the largest pebbles are at the south end, and a native Portlander coming ashore in his boat in fog can tell by their size how far he is from home.

Apart from the obvious dangers of the rocky bluff of Portland, another freak of nature is caused by the tides from West Bay and Weymouth Bay meeting off the Bill. The former reaches a tremendous force as it runs over the ledges at six or seven knots for nine or more hours of every twelve, and where it meets the latter, about a mile off the Bill, the dreaded Portland Race is formed. Another large area of confused waters is caused by the Shambles Bank, lying roughly south-east of the Bill. Although there is a channel between the Shambles and the mainland most vessels of any size pass both race and bank in a wide sweep when making for Portland or Weymouth.

An early wreck is recorded for Wyke Regis in December 1641, the *Golden Grape*, bound from Cadiz for Dover, when seven were drowned and thirteen saved. The inevitable local tale of a 'treasure ship' dates from 1765 and alludes to the Dutch East-Indiaman *Hoop* which sank off Fleet with bullion and jewels said to be worth more than £50,000. In the same gale the tobacco ship *Squirrel* stranded near Abbotsbury and the French frigate *Zénobie* went ashore at Chesil Cove.

A search through *Lloyd's Lists* between 1784 and 1824 reveals a full two hundred casualties in the Portland and Weymouth areas. However, in the days before Portland Breakwater was built it is difficult to be sure which side of Chesil Beach was meant by 'Portland Beach'. The bays on each side of the ridge were used for shelter in the appropriate conditions, but the commercial traffic for the communities of Portland would have to approach from the east.

The local type of boat at Portland is the lerrit or lerret, six-oared and clench-built, without rudder and normally without sail, evolved through the centuries as the most suitable design for launching from and hauling up the steep pebble ridge in any weather. The Portlanders were as adept at handling them as an eskimo in a kayak, but nowadays the fishing fleet is greatly reduced and carried on with more or less conventional motor boats. One interesting oddity was the Portlander's superstition that it was unlucky to put to sea without a pebble with a natural hole. Invariably the boats carried such a pebble attached to the stem-post by a short length of twine. The lerrets were frequently used for life-saving and one early report of December 3rd 1792, stated that when a large ship was seen on fire three leagues to the west 'all the boats along the shore are gone off so we hope the people will be saved'.

That such a praiseworthy humanitarian attitude did not always prevail, however, is borne out by contemporary reports of a disaster which happened three years later. On November 17-18th 1795, the fleet of Rear Admiral Hugh Christian, bound for the West Indies and convoying a large number of heavily laden troop transports and merchantmen, was scattered by a great westerly gale. Although the fleet was very close to Torbay when the strong blow came they could not reach shelter there and were ordered to put about and return to Spithead. A short while later at least six merchantmen found themselves too far north and embayed in West Bay. There they anchored in a desperate bid to keep off the beach, but all either foundered or were driven ashore and wrecked. Of the troop transports the *Piedmont* was lost with the greater part of her complement, but part of the crew and troops were saved from the *Venus*. All were saved from the ship *Hannah* with ordnance stores, but only a part of the crew of the *Aeolus* with masts and naval stores. The merchantman *Golden Grove*, with the

usual general cargo of European goods for the settlers and their planta-
tions, was pounded to pieces, as also the *Thomas* which, unlike the rest,
was not bound for the West Indies but had taken advantage of the
convoy for her passage to Oporto. A witness afterwards wrote that
three of them went to pieces in an hour near Wyke, and only fifteen
persons were saved. Others were wrecked farther up the beach. The
count of bodies washed ashore was 275, so that the total death roll
must have been considerably greater.

This witness wrote:—'To give a true description of the scenes of
horror I have been witness to would be impossible . . . Consider a
transport with near two hundred troops on board sinking within fifty
yards of the shore, the cries distinctly heard and the bodies floating on
the waves, but the means of affording assistance unpracticable. Of the
two hundred, ten lives are saved by the waves throwing the bodies on
the beach . . . But instead of the spectators (who are chiefly people from
Portland, who are always praying for wrecks on their coast) attempting
to rescue the drowning wretches their whole attention was devoted to
plunder and I was myself witness to a scene the most unpardonable that
ever humanity shuddered at. The body of an officer was driven on shore
and a party of the Portland people ran to it for the purpose of plunder,
a chest, however, coming ashore at the instant, the body was left to be
washed back by the next wave, while the inhuman wretches were solely
intent on preserving the chest. The officer, however, was saved by one
of our people and is now living.'

Some other disastrous early wrecks may be noted. In 1797 the London
West-Indiaman *Marquis of Worcester*, homeward bound from St.
Vincents, was thrown ashore near Weymouth and only one of her large
complement saved. In the following year the Liverpool ship *Duchess
of York* was lost with all hands on the rocks of the Bill. Neither of
these carried many passengers, but the next great loss in this area was
an East-Indiaman. On February 5th 1805, the *Earl of Abergavenny*, of
about 1,200 tons—a large ship for those days—outward bound from
London for Bengal and China, struck the Shambles, slipped off the
shoal and sank in twelve fathoms. Her captain, a brother of the poet
Wordsworth, and about three hundred others were drowned.

This loss was indeed one of the major catastrophes of our sea history.
She had sailed from Portsmouth on February 1st 1805, with four other
vessels in a convoy protected by the *Weymouth* frigate. Encountering
strong and unfavourable winds the fleet was separated from the frigate
on the first night out and in obedience to signalled instructions from

The French ketch St. Michael *was driven ashore a mile east of Lyme Regis on January 31st 1937 after her motor had broken down and most of her sails had been blown away. Her crew were helped ashore by coastguards and others.*

The experimental inshore rescue Boat X.5, designed and built by the pupils af Atlantic College, was stationed at Lyme Regis for a trial period during 1968. [*Photo: R.N.L.I.*]

The Swedish ketch Alioth, *after leaving West Bay harbour without a pilot, was driven on to the East Beach in light airs on May 13th 1923* [*Photo: Bridport Museum*]

The spritsail barge Lancelot, *of Rochester, stranded at West Bay while bound for Exeter with cement in November 1909* [*Photo: Bridport Museum*]

the commodore ship *Wexford*, they took pilots and made for the shelter of Portland Roads. At about 3 p.m. on the 4th, pilots were taken aboard for resuming the voyage, but the *Earl of Abergavenny* drove on the Shambles due to 'the ebb tide setting in fast and a slack wind'. Captain John Wordsworth at first thought she would be got off when the tide turned and for an hour and a half no alarm guns were fired. Then the carpenter discovered a leak and to make matters even more serious the wind increased to a gale. The water rapidly gained on the pumps and the ship began to settle on the sands. The purser was sent ashore in one of the boats with the ship's papers and despatches, the third mate, who happened to be Captain Wordsworth's cousin, and six seamen going with him. Not until about nine o'clock were the passengers told the true situation and by then it was difficult to keep order among the sailors. Some of these were demanding entry to the spirit room and it was necessary to mount an armed guard on the door. One shore boat came out taking three men and two lady passengers back to Portland. By ten the water was above the orlop deck and incredibly, according to a newspaper report, 'the ship's boats were forgotten to be hoisted out'. Then at about eleven the ship gave a surge and went down 'almost in a moment', in twelve fathoms. A large number of persons climbed the shrouds and others got into the long boat which floated off the deck, but although boats came to the scene in half an hour or so, and were hailed by those on the wreck, they did not save a soul. The seas breaking over the masts and the cold which numbed the fingers took a terrible toll. At about midnight, a sloop came up, commanded by a more determined master, and took off the pitiful remainder which, because they were stronger and more used to the cold, were all sailors and troops, not a single passenger being left. It is said the sloop made three trips and brought to safety about 60 men.

As to the reckoning; there had been about four hundred people on board, of which sixty were passengers, 160 were King's or East India Company's troops, and there were also thirty Chinese who were probably servants or stewards. About 124 were saved, made up of seven officers, five midshipmen, 73 crew, five passengers, and 34 troops. Captain Wordsworth was nicknamed 'The Philosopher' 'so cool a temperature was his disposition,' but on this occasion perhaps a more energetic master might have been preferable. Soon after the foundering the ship's spar deck rose under the pressure and released the baggage, which was washed ashore in all directions. The masts and yards were salved and taken to Weymouth. It was thought impossible to save the cargo, but a report of there being £70,000 in specie was a powerful stimulant and in the coming months much was saved, mainly by the use of diving bells made by 'the ingenious Mr. Tomkins'. Nearly a hundred bodies, including that of the Captain, were buried in a mass grave at Wyke churchyard.

Another disastrous wreck was on the night of March 26th 1815, when the East India 'Country Ship' *Alexander*, bound from Bombay for London, having been over five months on passage, was driven ashore near Wyke in a violent gale from the S.S.W. Only four lascars were saved out of a large crew, and one woman out of twenty passengers.

The first positive step to help shipping was the building of the high and low Portland lighthouses in 1789. Other steps followed slowly. Soon after the founding of the Life-boat Institution in March 1824, there was a move towards forming a Dorset Branch Association to provide lifeboats and life-saving apparatus. The need was then brutally underlined by a hurricane lasting the day and night of November 22-23rd 1824, which caused unparalleled havoc among shipping and in the coastal settlements: 'A tempest heavy with more frightful terrors is scarcely within the memory of man,' said the *Bristol Gazette*. The effect at Lyme has been noted already. In West Bay the Danish West-Indiaman *Carvalho*, laden with rum and cotton, was wrecked and all hands lost. At Fleet waves swept over the Chesil Beach, raising the level of the lagoon by 22 feet, then rushed into the little valley, destroying the whole village save the chancel of the church and a few adjoining cottages. Near Abbotsbury a Danish brig laden with fruit came ashore and by good fortune four of her crew of five were saved. At the southern end of the beach, at Chesil, eighty houses were swept away and thirty people drowned. Many fishing boats and their gear were lost and the *Colville* foundered a few yards off the beach—17 of 25 bodies which came to land were her crew and passengers. The Government sloop *Ebenezer*, with naval stores from Plymouth for Portsmouth, was washed high on the beach, where all were saved except the master. After the storm she was left so far from the sea on the western side that they were able, by superhuman efforts, to drag her to the Weymouth side and relaunch her. Near Weymouth the Dutch galliot *Johanna*, bound for Bordeaux, was driven against the rocks at Sandsfoot Castle with such force that her masts were thrown to the shore, enabling her crew to scramble to land at once. A vessel of about 500 tons was seen to founder with no survivors and was never identified. Off Osmington the Portsmouth smack *Sally* was driven against the anchored brig *Nancy*. As the two vessels lay momentarily locked together the son of the *Sally's* captain leaped on board the brig but, the two vessels then parting, the rest of the crew were swept away and drowned when the smack foundered. The *Nancy* was totally dismasted but rode out the gale. At Weymouth the quays were flooded, the north pier of the harbour nearly demolished, the esplanade breached, and the lower parts of houses flooded. The seas came over the neck of land and joined up with the backwater, leaving the town as an island.

After such a tale of disaster small wonder that determined efforts were made to introduce better means of life-saving. The Dorset Branch Association collected funds and with the aid of the parent institution, Plenty of Newbury was commissioned to build one of his 20-feet six-oared lifeboats which were then the approved model. There being some delay at the boatbuilding yard through a shortage of carpenters they in fact received a boat of the same size and type which had been built for Dungeness. She arrived early in 1826 and at about the same time, with Government help, Manby mortar apparatus was provided at Lulworth Cove, Osmington, Chesil Cove, Fleet and Abbotsbury.

It was an auspicious beginning but, unfortunately, as at so many other early lifeboat stations, the mere presence of a lifeboat was not sufficient to ensure an efficient life-saving service. Exercises were neglected and in cases of wreck the Portlanders preferred to use their own boats. The Dorset Branch Association appears to have become moribund by 1838 and the lifeboat was so neglected that by 1850 the *Northumberland Report* said her 'air boxes are warped and leaking; she is not worth repair'. In fact it was ascertained that she had never been used to save life and so in January 1851 she was sold to the highest bidder, fetching £2 'less three-pence for a postal order'.

There had been wrecks and rescues in this quarter century, of course. On December 14th 1825, the *Vigilant* had been wrecked at Lulworth, but in spite of the utmost efforts of Lieutenant Prior, R.N., and his Coastguard crew, only one man was saved. The official citation said 'Owen Lloyd in particular manifested great alacrity in throwing the rope by which Thomas Parker, the mate, was saved and drawn up the high cliff . . . Lieutenant Prior had risen from a sick bed to give the necessary directions to his men on the occasion. Parker was the only man saved, the vessel having almost immediately gone to pieces.' Lloyd received the Institution's silver medal and a sum of money was distributed among the crew.

Next, on February 23rd 1830, the Royal Mail steam packet *Meteor*, bound for Weymouth from the Channel Islands, ran on the rocks at Church Hope, Portland, in thick fog. Her mate, Edward Thresher, distinguished himself by scrambling to the shore over the slippery rocks and through his efforts every one of the passengers and crew were saved by means of ropes. Then on the following night, more than a hundred Portlanders swarmed aboard and pilfered a large proportion of the baggage. Another wreck mentioned in the Institution's records for this period was early in 1842, when the brig *Amyntas*, of Exeter, was driven ashore at Weymouth, John Hansford won the silver medal for dashing into the surf and dragging ashore two of the dazed and half-frozen crew.

Another great cyclonic storm visited the Weymouth area in the last days of November 1838. The press said 'It is not in the recollection of the oldest inhabitant to have witnessed such a continuance of heavy and violent gales of wind from the north-east, east and south-east as we have experienced since Sunday morning (November 25th) until Thursday afternoon, attended during Monday and Tuesday with sudden and powerful squalls of rain and hail, and during Wednesday and Thursday with vivid lightning and tremendous peals of thunder.' On the night of the 27th the French brig *Maria Louisa* was thrown ashore near Preston Cliff and was soon 'a perfect wreck'—to quote the contemporary description. Of her crew of five, four were saved. The master had suffered a broken leg by a blow from the main boom and was got ashore with great difficulty. A preventive man took out a rope and a plank and after a long persevering struggle brought ashore two boys. On the night of Wednesday to Thursday the whole Portland Beach, nearly to Bridport 'was one continued scene of distress and misery, it was strewed with broken boxes, furniture, fragments of clothes, utensils, trunks and pieces of wreck.' Nine vessels were driven ashore or foundered. The schooner *Columbine* went to pieces and all hands were lost; from another schooner there was only one survivor, and the *Dove*, of Weymouth, with groceries, was another wreck. It was said nearly a hundred lives were lost but only one body cast up. Even the Fleet lagoon was whipped to foam and a boat returning from the beach to the mainland upset, drowning three men. A Coastguard was killed by lightning as he stood on the beach and there was a greater surf than had ever been known before.

In 1849 the first stone of the Portland Breakwater was laid by the Prince Consort, so inaugurating a great work which has helped to save many seafaring lives over the years. It was completed in 1872 and then comprised two moles totalling a mile and a half, the outer one detached to provide an entry. Between 1894 and 1903 a further breakwater and another detached portion were built out from the northern shore at Bincleaves, and these totalled two miles. As a harbour of refuge it is, of course, less frequently used than in the days of trading sail, and during the First World War the southernmost of the three entrances was blocked for defence purposes.

Another great help to navigators was the Shambles light-vessel, established in 1859 and stationed east of the shoal, about 5½ miles east of the Bill. The two Portland lighthouses were abandoned in favour of one new tower, nearer the Bill, in 1867.

Among casualties of the 1850's and 1860's there was a daring rescue in the midst of Portland Race on March 8th 1857, when the *patron* of the Honfleur fishing smack *Victoire Desirée* took his vessel through the boiling waters to save the three-man crew of the Lyme Regis smack *Hope*, which had foundered in a sudden squall. Pierre Picard thus joined the small but distinguished band of Frenchmen who have won the Institution's silver medal. The Breakwater itself was the scene of a wreck on January 30th 1861, when the Plymouth schooner *Norval* was thrown on to the stonework in a gale. Joseph White and William Flann led a crew of six local men which put off in a shore boat and at considerable risk saved the crew of five, so in turn earning silver medals.

These and other casualties prompted the R.N.L.I. in 1868 to survey the area for a lifeboat station. Portland was again considered but it was decided that Weymouth would better cover the north and east sides of the bay. A boathouse was built on the south side of the harbour and a slipway cut through the quay, the needs of pedestrians being met by a removable bridge across the gap. The whole station, house and lifeboat, was given by the Earl of Strafford. The boat was a 33-feet self-righter with ten oars, named *Agnes Harriet*. Normally she did not employ a carriage, but for the formal inauguration on January 26th 1869, she was drawn through the streets to the Esplanade by six fine grey horses in a colourful procession of local dignitaries and representatives of uniformed bodies.

Almost immediately after the opening of the Weymouth station a movement was begun at Portland to obtain their own lifeboat. The fishermen were particularly keen, but they wanted a boat of their own choice—a lerret, which must be built by the established builder Joseph Talbot, of Wyke. They would allow it to be fitted with air cases, but they wanted nothing to do with life-jackets, saying they could not row in them. Possibly this was a case of lack of shoulder room in a small craft, for every lifeboatman elsewhere soon learned to cope with this clumsy but essential item of equipment. The Institution envisaged a station on Chesil Beach—very useful indeed for a quick launch into West Bay—which would be an auxiliary to the Weymouth station and managed by the same committee. It would, of course, have to comply with the Institution's rules which were drawn up in order to ensure as high a degree of safety as possible. Boats modelled on local craft were in use elsewhere and they were quite willing to provide a boat of lerret type so long as it had essential safety features incorporated. Unfortunately, as borne out by contemporary newspaper reports, there was some degree of mistrust between the Portlanders and the Weymouth committee. It was a rekindling of the historic rivalries between the Islanders and the 'Kimberlins' and unfortunately the upshot was that Portland never got its lifeboat.

Astonishingly, Weymouth lifeboat, in spite of eight service launches, did not accomplish a rescue until her ninth, a fortnight or so before she was replaced in 1887. Meanwhile a number of wrecks, some tragic in the extreme, had occurred in the area. The iron ship *Royal Adelaide*, of Liverpool, was wrecked on Chesil Beach on the night of November 25th 1872. She was bound for Sydney with between thirty and forty emigrants and on the night of the 24th they had passed Portland light close on the starboard bow. Proceeding down channel, they met increasingly bad weather. In the early hours of the 25th they turned back to seek shelter but went off course in thick blinding rain squalls. During the afternoon they found themselves embayed in West Bay and on approaching Chesil Beach were warned off by the Coastguards burning blue lights. However they could not wear away satisfactorily. Rolling heavily and quite unmanageable, the ship was driven back on to the beach. Her back broke in a few hours and her masts fell, but meanwhile frantic efforts were made to save her crew and passengers. The mate first tried to swim ashore with a line but was drowned. The Coastguard then got a rocket line in place but the passengers were afraid to trust themselves to the basket. In desperation the captain seized one of the children, got into the basket and was safely pulled ashore. He wanted to go back but was prevented. Several others came ashore safely by this means, but then a woman seized with panic grasped a rope in the rigging as she was being swung over the rail, was dragged out of the basket and dropped into the sea to be seen no more. About eight had been saved when the mizen mast fell and the rocket line was rendered useless. A crowd of spectators, estimated at 3,000, were then forced to watch as the last handful of the crew and passengers were washed away one by one.

On the night of September 11th 1877, fifteen miles South-by-west of Portland Bill, at the height of a force-8 gale, there was a disastrous collision between the iron ship *Avalanche*, of Southampton, and the ship *Forest*, of Windsor, Nova Scotia. The *Avalanche* was outward bound, having left London for Wellington, New Zealand, on the 8th, with a general cargo, mainly Manchester goods, valued between £75,000 and £100,000, 35 crew and 63 passengers, of whom eight were children. She was without her figurehead which was lost in a collision with a foreign barque in the Thames as she set out. The more superstitious among her sailors probably read an omen in this unfortunate mishap. The *Forest* was also outward bound from London, but on passage for Sandy Hook in ballast, with a crew of 21. The night was unusually dark with drizzling rain, high seas and a strong wind. At about 9.30, when the *Avalanche* was on the port tack and the *Forest* on the starboard tack some twelve miles off the Bill, the *Forest* struck the *Avalanche* between the main and mizen masts, rebounded and struck again farther aft. In less than five minutes the *Avalanche* gave three plunges and sank. By the rule of the sea the *Forest* had the right of way and her master burnt a flare to warn the *Avalanche*, but to no purpose. The *Forest* was so damaged and leaky—she became full to the tween decks—that a quarter of an hour after the collision her master decided to abandon ship and all got away in three boats. In the confusion some were left behind but it was impossible to return alongside to take them off. They did pick up some men from the *Avalanche*, but in the rough weather during the night one boat was overwhelmed and washed up later on Chesil Beach containing only five bodies. Another boat was never seen again. The third boat was seen at daybreak off Chesil Beach but her occupants were afraid to attempt a landing. Two Portland lerrets were launched, each with a crew of seven, and brought to shore the twelve survivors. The whole of the passengers and 32 of the crew of the *Avalanche* were found to be missing at the final count. The *Forest* lost twelve men and her wreckage was washed up in large quantities at Chesil Cove. As a memorial to the lost, relatives and friends collected sufficient funds to build St. Andrew's Church, Southwell, which was opened for worship two years later.

There was another collision off Portland on September 6th 1882, when an unknown Dutch galliot sank with all hands after collision with the Liverpool barque *Comadre* in a north-easterly gale. In the following year, on June 22nd 1883, there was yet another disastrous collision off the Bill between two iron-built full-rigged ships belonging to the New Zealand Shipping Company, both bound for Wellington. The *Waitara* and the *Hurunui* left London together, and dismissing pilots and tugs, beat down the Channel against a gentle south-westerly wind. In the evening of June 22nd they passed through a rain storm and then out of it at about ten o'clock, but were left in somewhat misty conditions. The two ships were on opposite tacks and it was the duty of the *Waitara*, on the port tack, to keep clear of her sister vessel, but this she did not do. The *Hurunui*, travelling at a considerable speed, struck the *Waitara* on her starboard side. After a brief recoil, the wind being still in her sails, she struck a second time and the *Waitara* sank in little more than two minutes. She had on board a crew of 25, 16 passengers and a stowaway, and of these 14 crew, including the second officer who was on watch, and 12 passengers were drowned. The *Hurunui*, saved by the strength of her forward watertight bulkhead, at once lowered boats and by this means the survivors were saved.

Of the several strandings on the Chesil Beach in this period the most spectacular was the Norwegian barque *Christiana* on September 2nd 1883. She was bound from her home port of Drammen, with a cargo of flooring boards, for Dartmouth. She was thrown ashore at Chesil Cove in a storm of hurricane strength, two of her crew of ten being lost. The schooner *Sapphire*, coal-laden, had been wrecked at Chesil Cove on the evening of August 8th, her whole crew being saved by the rocket apparatus. Then on the evening of August 27th the paddle passenger steamer *Bournemouth*, bringing back 197 passengers from a day's outing to Torquay, ran ashore in dense fog between the Bill and the high lighthouse. All were saved by the ship's boats and others which came to the scene, some being landed at Chesil, where one boat capsized in the waves and a number of passengers got a wetting, while others were taken round the Bill to be landed at Southwell.

On January 18th 1887, the Norwegian steamship *Nor*, bound from Cadiz for Bergen with salt, was driven ashore on the Chesil Beach. All hands were saved by the rocket apparatus, but the steamer quickly broke in two and became a total wreck. The *Agnes Harriet* accomplished her one rescue on November 1st following. During the morning several vessels were reported being driven out of Portland Roads, then protected only by the southern breakwater, by a gale of hurricane force from the S.S.W., accompanied by heavy rain and hail. The lifeboat crew stood by and at nine o'clock the brigantine *Maren*, of Fano in Denmark, bound from Mexico with logwood for Hamburg, was seen to be dragging her anchors rapidly. There was grave danger she would strike the Mixens or perhaps the outer pier, and accordingly the lifeboat was launched at once. Arriving close to the brigantine they stood by while she drove past the harbour clear of immediate danger, but so fast was she dragging that the lifeboatmen were hard pressed to keep up with her, the boat being filled several times by heavy seas. They arrived alongside at about 10.30 and the *Maren*'s captain was advised to pay out all possible cable to stop her dragging, but this was of no avail. An hour later she struck the ground some distance from the shore in the midst of broken water. Despite two appeals her crew would not leave and then, as the tide fell, the weather moderated a little, leaving the vessel lying safely. The lifeboat returned so that her crew could get some food and dry clothing, but in the early afternoon it blew strongly again so they went off a second time. On this occasion the Danes wanted to be taken off and after several attempts the lifeboat got alongside. After taking off the seven men they returned to the harbour with a long hard pull into the teeth of the gale.

A couple of weeks later a new 34-feet self-righting lifeboat, the *Friern Watch*, arrived at the station. She was also fitted for ten oars, but was of the latest design with tanks for water ballast. She was the gift of E. Homan, of Finchley, the unusual name being that of his house, which had formerly been the watch-gate to a friary. The inaugural ceremony on December 6th was a colourful affair watched by ten thousand spectators. Of course, Weymouth, as a coastal garrison town with close connections with the Navy, Army and Merchant Navy could always muster an almost unlimited number of uniformed figures. The procession was formed at the Guild Hall. It was headed by the brass band of H.M.S. *Boscawen*, followed by detachments of the Royal Navy, the Marine Artillery, the Royal Naval Reserve Volunteers, the lifeboat crew, then two open carriages with Mrs. and the three Misses Homan, the Mayoress and other ladies, then Captains Cosens, Parker, Renouf and Lefevre—the much respected commanders of the steam mail packets—followed by police, serjeants-of-mace, the corporation and magistrates. All ships were decorated and the majestic two-funnelled packet *Aquila* fired a salute. It was indeed an ambitious show to organise, especially in an English December.

Not long afterwards the *Friern Watch* performed what turned out to be her only rescue. Late in the evening of November 25th 1888, the Welsh schooner *Mary Davies* was seen drifting before a strong south-westerly gale towards a lee shore. The seas were heavy and the weather thick, and it was fortunately decided to send the lifeboat off. She arrived alongside just as the schooner's crew were preparing to light a flare. The three men were taken off and put on board the steam tug *Queen*, which was nearby, and the tug then towed the lifeboat back to harbour. Tugs were often called to help the lifeboat at Weymouth, but it was not until 1897 that their services were put on a regular footing by an agreement to pay a minimum of £3 for a daytime call, and £6 by night.

Possibly the youngest person ever to receive the R.N.L.I. silver medal was Frederick Carter, a lad of eleven years who, with Frank Perry, aged sixteen, were rowing their boat in smooth water in the harbour mouth on May 26th 1890. Suddenly their attention was drawn to another boat which was in difficulties in the midst of surf out in the bay where the strong easterly breeze was being felt. As they watched the boat was capsized and its two occupants thrown into the sea. Without stopping to think of the very real danger to themselves of being swamped in the broken water, the two lads pulled manfully to the spot and were able to rescue one of the two men. Both lads were awarded the silver medal.

The first *Friern Watch* had twelve service launches, but only one was successful. Meanwhile Chesil Beach and the west side of Portland had continued to take its toll. On March 8th 1888, the iron barque *Lanoma*, of London, homeward bound with wool and hides from Launceston, Tasmania, stranded, and twelve of her crew of eighteen were drowned. On March 8th 1889 the Hull steamer *Vera* stranded near Langton. Her crew of 25, with three passengers and two stowaways from the Mediter-ranean, were helped ashore by coastguards.

On April 21st 1890, the French barque *Ehen*, bound from Bremen for Bordeaux with rice and pickles, drifted on to the rocks near the Bill in a light breeze, her crew of ten and single passenger being fortunately able to reach the shore in their boats. On October 31st 1890, there was a spectacular stranding when the Austrian schooner *Fannie C.*, bound from Hamburg for Buenos Aires with general cargo, was put ashore at Chesil while on fire. She became a total loss, but her crew of ten were saved. On January 2nd 1891, the Penzance steamer *Thames*, bound from Newlyn for London with a cargo of roadstone and tin ingots was wrecked on Tor Rocks, Chesil Cove, in foggy weather, her crew of twelve escaping. Then on October 13th in the same year the Norwegian brig *Ora et Labora*, bound from Sweden for Nantes with deals drove ashore at Chesil Cove in a severe gale, the Coastguard saving her crew of seven. There were two more total wrecks in 1894, the first on March 5th, when the schooner *Lord Duffus*, of Inverness, bound from St. Domingo for London with mahogany logs, was wrecked near the Bill with the loss of her whole crew of six. The second, on August 26th, the steamship *Gertrude*, of West Hartlepool, bound from Huelva for Rotterdam with iron pyrites, stranded in fog at Blacknor Point. Fortunately, in calm weather, the whole of her crew of eighteen and two passengers were saved.

These casualties, all close inshore, were probably best left to the Coastguards for rescue purposes, but it was generally felt that Weymouth ought to have a lifeboat designed for sailing greater distances. Accordingly in 1903 it was decided to replace the first *Friern Watch* with one of the Watson-class, 38 feet long and nominally twelve-oared, which were then the last word in lifeboat design. She bore the same name as her predecessor, Mr. Homan having given a sum sufficient to endow the boat in perpetuity.

A few days before she arrived at Weymouth, however, there were two spectacular wrecks on Chesil Beach in quick succession. On the afternoon of Sunday October 25th 1903, the Russian schooner *Anna Maria* was seen in West Bay flying a signal of distress. She was bound from Teignmouth for Lisbon with china clay, but in a gale of 'force 9' from the south-south-west, with very heavy seas, had been blown helplessly across Lyme Bay. Of three tugs which went out to her aid, the *Petrel*, from Portland, got a line on board but it parted after two hours of towing. Then the *Petrel* received damage and had to return, leaving the *Anna Maria* anchored off Blacknor Point. After several hours rolling and pitching the schooner broke from her anchors and drove ashore on Chesil Beach at about nine in the evening. As she struck, her mainmast fell over the side and formed a bridge to the shore. Without waiting to save anything the six-man crew clambered over the mast to safety.

On the following day the Norwegian barque *Patria*, on passage from Frederickstad for Durban with a cargo of deals, encountered the same heavy south-westerly gale and was about to turn back to Portland Roads when a heavy squall blew away nearly all her sails. Left completely unmanageable, she could not round Portland Bill but was driven relentlessly into West Bay and soon went on the beach. The

Coastguard fired a rocket line over her, but the crew did not understand what to do. Two men jumped into the surf and after a desperate struggle were helped ashore by spectators who dashed into the waves. In the end the whole crew of eleven were saved although with one broken arm and one broken leg as unsolicited souvenirs. They had already lost a man overboard in an earlier squall in the Channel.

Returning to the new lifeboat *Friern Watch*, which arrived on station in late October 1903, she had to wait less than four months for her maiden service. During the day on February 26th 1904, a gale had raged and in the early evening the Coastguard reported a large German ship, the *Alanda*, was signalling for help. A quick launch was made in ten minutes, but on arrival near the ship four tugs were found in attendance. However, the master asked the coxswain to stand by as he was not sure the tugs would be successful in getting him into a safe position.

A year later, to the day, the Coastguard phoned the lifeboat secretary at 8 in the morning that a torpedo boat destroyer was in difficulty drifting rapidly towards the breakwater in a south-westerly hurricane and very heavy seas. The lifeboat crew were assembled, but at the last moment it was discovered that a tug had taken the naval vessel in tow. However, an hour later a further message came telling of a large barque in distress off the Shambles. She was said to have a heavy list, to have lost sails and that her crew were in the rigging with the seas breaking over them. A tug having been engaged, the lifeboat went out in tow and found the barque was the *County of Anglesea*, bound in ballast from Rouen for Liverpool. Her crew wanted to be taken off and one jumped down into the lifeboat. Another fell into the sea in his eagerness and was saved with difficulty. The barque's master then forbade any more men to leave. The lifeboat stood by through the night and on the next morning took lines to two other tugs which eventually towed the casualty to safety. She was then almost on her beam ends.

In the next few years there were other strandings on the west side of Portland, none of which involved loss of life, and only one of which became a total loss. The Blue Funnel liner *Patroclus*, from Brisbane with a cargo mainly of wool and skins, ran ashore in dense fog at Blacknor Point on September 13th 1907. Tugs could not move her and when it was found that her forehold had fifteen feet of water the reports became very pessimistic. However, four tugs and the Liverpool Salvage Association's famous ex-gunboat the *Linnet*, came to help, and they eventually refloated her on the evening of the 22nd with no less than eleven steam pumps working at top speed on her decks.

The next stranding was on Tor Rock on June 8th, 1910, when the German steamship *Okahandja*, bound from Carthagena for Stettin with oil, also lost her way in dense fog. The captain's wife and children landed in a ship's boat and the Coastguard rigged their apparatus, but the crew of 29 stayed on board. She was badly holed so a large part of her cargo was jettisoned in a night and day operation and she refloated on the evening of the 9th, with the help of the German salvage vessel *E. M. Svitzer*. First repairs were completed at Weymouth and she later went back to Germany.

The *Myrtledene*, of Newcastle, another ore steamer bound from Sagunto for Rotterdam, was not so lucky. She stranded at Mutton Cove on March 25th 1912, quickly filled with water and became a total wreck. Her crew of 24 and two passengers were saved by the Coast-guard.

After the outbreak of war the *Friern Watch* performed a fine service on December 11th 1914, when the crew were saved from the schooner *Ardente*, of Paimpol. Launched during the afternoon in a heavy south-easterly gale the lifeboat was towed out by a tug and found the schooner dragging her anchors in the bay. Attempts were made to take her in tow, but were foiled by the shallow water and her light condition. The lifeboat was then taken alongside under oars and in a blinding rain storm the five Frenchmen were rescued.

Several more launches were made during the war years although so many Weymouth men were in the services it was often difficult to make up a crew. It is recorded, for instance, that when they went out to H.M. hired armed trawler *Kildeer*, of Hull, on August 17th 1915, several soldiers volunteered to make up the crew. No service resulted from this launch, but there was a useful double service on November 18th 1916. At seven in the morning the steel barque *Gladys*, of Bristol, was seen to be dragging her anchors in a gale from east-north-east. The lifeboat went off through heavy seas and took off her crew of twenty as a precautionary measure. The large steel four-masted barque *Celticburn*, of Greenock, was in a similar position and in fact grounded in Wey-mouth Bay. Her crew of 28 were likewise landed. Later in the day the weather moderated and both barques were towed to safety, the lifeboat being launched a second time to reboard the crew of the *Celticburn*.

On the night of January 9-10th 1920, there was a tragedy at Kim-meridge when the Hain liner *Treveal*, bound from Calcutta for Dundee with jute, was wrecked. She had been driven off course by extremely heavy weather and struck the ledges at about nine in the evening. Her wireless calls were not received, possibly screened by the high cliffs, but someone did realise that something was amiss and the Portland tug *Pilot* was sent out to search. In the darkness she failed to find the casualty, however, and returned. Early on the morning of the 10th the tug *Petrel* towed out the *Friern Watch*, but when they got to the scene, some sixteen miles to the east, they found the wreck abandoned and beginning to break up with the seas breaking violently over her.

As conditions in the open lifeboat would be terrible when towing back against the gale they put in at Swanage for shelter and to report. It transpired that Captain Paynter had decided to abandon ship at nine in the morning and the crew got away in two boats containing 21 and 22 respectively. In the cauldron of seas at the foot of the cliffs both boats capsized and only seven men got ashore.

A few days after this disaster, on the 15th, there was another stranding at the Portland end of Chesil Beach. A week or so earlier the steamship *Preveza*, of Argostoli in the Greek island of Cephalonia, had collected bunkers and stores at Portland and then steamed to Cardiff for a cargo, but this had been refused as she was not insured. She was returning up the English Channel, bound for Rotterdam, when she became enveloped in dense fog and eventually grounded in Chesil Cove in the late afternoon. In her light condition she drove high up the ridge with the tide and in the comparatively calm seas this at least meant there was no immediate danger to life. News of the stranding quickly reached the shipping community and various tradesmen who had earlier supplied coal and stores but had not received payment, obtained writs which were formally 'nailed to the mast.' Early the next morning two Portland tugs, the *Pilot* and *Petrel*, attempted to tow her off at high tide, but the former fouled her screw with a towing line and the attempt had to be abandoned. The large London salvage vessel *Ellida* came round from Southampton but also failed after strenuous as well as ingenious attempts. A bank of shingle had by then built up to seaward of the casualty so the *Ellida* tried to pull her free stern-first in an oblique direction. This meant going very close inshore. The *Ellida* had dropped her anchor to ensure a means of retreat, but the cable broke under the strain and entangled with her screw so that she too was out of action. The winds were increasing and it looked as if there would be a second stranding, but the *Petrel*'s master boldly brought in his vessel and connected with the *Ellida*. He towed her seawards, heading into the strong westerly gale, but it was found she was held to her anchor just as tightly as if the wire had been made fast on deck and as it was underwater there was little chance of cutting her free. For two days and nights, rising and falling in the waves which were thundering towards the beach, the smaller tug held the larger clear of danger. Then the *Petrel*'s bunkers were nearly exhausted and she had to go back to Portland. The tow was taken over by Cosen's paddle tug *Albert Victor*. As luck would have it, soon after the fresh connection was made the wire rope snapped at last, no doubt as a result of the *Petrel*'s gallant 48-hours of tugging and straining, and the *Albert Victor* made an easy £3,000 salvage money by taking the *Ellida* round to Portland. Under 'no cure no pay' rules the *Petrel* got nothing. The *Preveza* broke in two a week or so later, and in the end had to be scrapped on the spot. Parts of her boilers are still to be seen when gales disturb the pebbles.

On the day after the *Preveza* stranding an Admiralty steam trawler, the *James Fennell*, bound from Gibraltar for Portsmouth, ran ashore on rocks nearby and became a total wreck. Such vessels were two a penny at the time, having been built in great numbers during the war, and probably nobody bothered very much about the loss of another standard trawler.

On October 5th 1920, the lifeboat carried out a difficult service to another small naval craft. The drifter attached to H.M.S. *Warspite* for stores, personnel and ammunition duties, stranded on the Mixen Reef in rough seas whipped up by a strong south-easterly breeze. The *Charles Deere James*, a reserve lifeboat temporarily on the station, was asked to stand by. She remained at hand in very unpleasant conditions until a tug got a hawser to the drifter and when she was refloated in a leaking state accompanied her into harbour in case she should suddenly founder.

For the last four years of her life the *Friern Watch* was kept fairly busy. In 1921 and 1922, she helped two of the high-rigged Thames-type spritsail barges which used to lend colour to the scene in the Channel. On September 18th 1921, it was the *Cecilia*, bound from Ghent for Bridport with basic slag (fertiliser), disabled in a moderate easterly gale with steering gear trouble and lost sails. As was the usual practice with these craft the skipper had his wife with him— a very active member of the crew—and all five were quite exhausted with their struggle with the elements. The *Cecilia* was in an awkward position off the Blacknor, on the west of Portland, but several lifeboatmen were put on board and tugs arrived on the scene later. In the difficult conditions caused by the Portland Race she was eventually brought round to the safety of Portland Harbour. The second 'sprittie' was the *Savoy*, of Dover, which had lost her principal sails on April 1st 1922, when bound from Cherbourg for Cowes. A tug towed her to Weymouth from off the Bill, with the lifeboat in attendance.

Later in 1922, four days before Christmas, there was an arduous service in which they saved the crew of the Danish schooner *Meta*, of Troense, on the Island of Taasinge. Bound up-channel, the schooner was in difficulties in a heavy south-westerly gale. On receipt of a message from the Coastguard the lifeboat and tugs went off, but so bad was the weather the tugs had to put back. The Coxswain later signalled to the Coastguard at the Bill that he could not round the point, so he was also recalled. Four hours later the *Meta* was reported as having drifted past the Bill in an easterly direction. Going out again, the lifeboat was then able to come up to her and rescue her seven-man crew.

The difficulty of taking people from the detached portions of Portland Breakwater was demonstrated during the night of February 22-23rd 1923, when the small steamer *Craigside* and the ketch *Phoenix* were both blown ashore on to the pell-mell blocks of granite in a whole north-westerly gale. The crews scrambled on to the breakwater but heavy seas were breaking right over and cascading down the inner side making it extremely uncomfortable and dangerous to remain there. In the prevailing conditions the lifeboat and several other craft found they could not reach the men. However, at four in the morning the weather moderated somewhat and twelve men were brought ashore. Unfortunately the skipper of the *Phoenix* had been drowned when she became holed and sank.

During 1923 it was announced that as soon as the new lifeboat was ready for the Spurn Point station, at the mouth of the Humber, the *Samuel Oakes*, a 40-feet Watson-type motor lifeboat, only six years old, would be transferred to Weymouth. She arrived in April 1924, having already saved 25 persons and eight vessels. She was at Weymouth five years and had sixteen service launches, ten of which resulted in services and in three of which lives were saved, totalling nine. The coming of the motor lifeboat necessitated a new house with an electric winch and workshop space. The cost of about £5,000 was partly met by collections at the cinemas of the Albany Ward circuit.

The first motor lifeboat services at Weymouth were on January 1st and 2nd 1925, to the French brigantine *La Servannaise*. She had been at anchor in a heavy south-westerly gale off Redcliff Point, but had dragged across the bows of a steamer and the two anchor chains had become locked together. Her bowsprit was carried away and she was

The paddle steamer Bournemouth *stranded on the west side of Portland Bill in dense fog on August 27th 1886 when returning from Torquay. All the passengers were saved but the vessel became a total wreck.* [*Photo: Eric Latcham Collection*]

The Norwegian steamship Nor *stranded on Chesil Beach in January 1887 and became a wreck. All hands were saved by the rocket apparatus.*

[*Photo: Eric Latcham Collection*]

The French barque Ehen *stranded on the west side of Portland Bill in April 1890.*
[*Photo: Eric Latcham Collection*]

Stranded on March 18th 1889, the steamship Vera *became a total wreck on the Chesil Bank near Langton Herring. Her crew, passengers and stowaways, totalling 30, were saved by the coastguards.* [*Photo: Eric Latcham Collection*]

partly dismasted in the collision. On the first launch the lifeboat stood by while a tug freed the two vessels, but on the next day, the gale still blowing, it was necessary for her to stand by for a further period in case the Frenchman should drive on the rocks. She was eventually towed into Weymouth on the morning of the 3rd.

The services of the *Samuel Oakes* will be found in the service record. Occasions when there was actual saving of life were in September 1925, when four were rescued from the schooner *Duchess* which, in ballast, was being so thrown about by a heavy south-westerly gale that her crew feared she would founder at any moment. However, she did survive and the next day a tug took her into Portland harbour. In the case of the motor boat *Rose Mary* in November 1926, the three persons on board had abandoned their craft when her engines broke down, but they were seen and rescued only just in time as their small dinghy was almost swamped. The lifeboat, having taken the three on board, was able to tow the *Rose Mary* back to harbour. The *Bonnie Jean*, in June 1928, was unmanageable in a moderate gale, but fortunately the lifeboat could tow her and her two occupants to safety.

On February 8th 1926, there was a tragedy in Weymouth Bay when Coxswain William Tizard and Assistant Mechanic William Duignan went out in a small boat to pilot into Weymouth the collier *Opal*, which had arrived from Goole. Their boat capsized in the rough seas whipped up by the south-easterly gale almost immediately they left the shelter of the harbour piers. The Coastguard called out the lifeboat, whose crew did not know they were searching for their comrades, but although the area was lit by H.M.S. *Tiger*'s searchlight no trace could be found of the two men.

In 1929 a new motor lifeboat was built for Weymouth. She was the gift of the Royal Mail and Union Castle Steamship Company, and named *Lady Kylsant* after the wife of their Chairman. This lifeboat was the first of the latest version of the former 40-feet craft. She was 40½-feet long, had twin engines and screws, a radius of action of 117 miles at cruising speed, and could take 160 persons on board before the deck became awash. On what was probably her first local practice run, July 22nd 1929, she was able to save two sailors from the visiting U.S. Fleet who were drifting helplessly to sea on the tidal currents in a small boat. This service, although reported in the press, does not appear on the official list. The first on the list came on August 26th following, when she went round the Bill to West Bay to help the steamship *Jolly Esmond*. While on passage from Jersey for London with granite, this small steamer had gone aground on a rocky ledge in calm but hazy weather. The lifeboat was able to lay out a kedge anchor by which means the steamer pulled herself clear when the tide rose.

January 12th 1930 saw moments of near panic as the small Cardiff collier *Forester* drove before a whole westerly gale right through the Atlantic fleet moored in Portland Harbour. Ricocheting from one taut anchor cable to another she seemed to bear a charmed life until she crashed on to the stonework of the breakwater, slid off, and turned turtle. She had been on a ballast passage from Poole for Swansea when she came in to shelter from the gale. Her crew of six and a young stowaway were lucky to be able to scramble, wet and frozen, on to the breakwater from the almost upturned hull. Getting them into the lifeboat proved far more difficult than it seemed and in the end two lifeboatmen had to get on to the breakwater to arrange the rope tackle by which they were saved.

On September 19th 1930, the *Lady Kylsant* was called out by the Coastguard to save the crew of two of the Malouin ketch *Leonie* which had been bound from Poole for Roscoff in ballast, but was now ashore under Sandsfoot Castle. In spite of the south-westerly gale, heavy seas and rain, the service took less than an hour. On the next day the Coastguard reported a vessel drifting to sea from the direction of Portland and the lifeboat, again launched, found her to be the *Leonie*, which had slid off the rocks little damaged, and towed her back to Weymouth. While this was happening the large French three-masted schooner *Madeleine Tristran* was being driven ashore at Chesil Cove where the full force of the heavy gale was being felt. She was one of the 'Grand Bankers' which fished the Newfoundland Banks, being mother ships for fleets of one-man dories, but on this occasion was on a coasting voyage from Treguier for Havre with 52 tons of gin. Her crew of seven got ashore with help from people on the beach, but the vessel was eventually thrown out of reach of the waves. Immensely strongly built, her partly stripped hull was a landmark for several years until she was broken up by the council as a source of rat infestation.

Although the *Lady Kylsant* made eight service launches and saved nine lives in sixteen months it was realised that the true needs of the Weymouth station would only be met by one of the largest type of lifeboat then being built—the 51-feet Barnett class. The extra power would enable her to cope far better with the extraordinarily strong tides around Portland and the severe gales which periodically visit this area of the Channel. In November 1930, the *William and Clara*

Ryland, one of two lifeboats provided from the legacy of a Sheffield gentleman, arrived on the station and the *Lady Kylsant* was transferred to Howth in Ireland. The new lifeboat had a delayed inaugural ceremony on July 16th 1932, when she was formally dedicated by the Bishop of Salisbury and named by the Countess of Shaftesbury.

After a launch in June 1932, leading to a long unavailing search in fog for the motor fishing boat *Sleuth Hound*—which reached safety unaided—the new lifeboat's first rescue call came on the following September 8th. The Coastguard had for some time been keeping a sailing vessel in West Bay under observation as she had lost her headsails. Soon after one o'clock in the afternoon she showed distress signals and the lifeboat was called out in a moderate gale from the S.S.W., with rough sea and heavy rain coming in squalls. Rounding Portland Bill she found the vessel to be a former pilot cutter, now the yacht *Hope*. Besides having lost some sails her engine had broken down and she was drifting helplessly. After waiting awhile for the right tidal conditions for returning round the Bill, the lifeboat towed the yacht and her crew of four back to Weymouth.

Oddly enough the next service, on March 11th following, was to the Lyme Regis sailing and pulling lifeboat *Thomas Masterman Hardy*, which had left her station on the previous day—it being now closed— and was heading for Weymouth where she was to be put on the railway for the London storeyard. Attempting to round the Bill in the teeth of a strong easterly breeze she was delayed and when the tide turned she was unable to make headway. The Weymouth lifeboat towed her to harbour.

On the night of February 16th 1936, they were called to the assistance of the largest vessel in the service record so far—the 20,109-ton *Winchester Castle*, of the Union Castle Line. Homeward bound from Durban for Southampton, she had been set a little northward by the West Bay indraught and in poor visibility grounded under Blacknor Fort on the west side of Portland. The lifeboat stood by for a part of the night, but the liner was in a position sheltered from the south-easterly wind and after a while it was realised there was no danger to life. The liner was later refloated.

On analysis most casualties were to the south and west of Weymouth, but on February 25th 1937, the *Ryland* was called eastwards to the vicinity of Lulworth Cove where the small London motor vessel *Gertruda* was being helplessly driven shorewards with her engines out of order.

Another service was unusual in that the skipper of the yacht *Gisèle Aimée* was the coxswain of the St. Malo lifeboat enjoying a cruise to Portsmouth while on leave. Early on the morning of August 4th 1938, the yacht came into Weymouth Bay but her engine broke down at a crucial moment and she was gradually driven ashore north of the pier. The reserve lifeboat *Alfred and Clara Heath* was on duty at the time and went out at 4.30 in the morning, but although she got a line on board could not drag the yacht clear. It was obvious they would have to wait until the tide flowed again. While the lifeboat was standing by a thunder storm struck the area, reported to be the worst in living memory. The yacht was pulled free at about two in the afternoon and brought to moorings, in a leaky state, in Weymouth harbour.

The war came early to the Weymouth station with a call on the evening of September 15th 1939. Four ship's boats were reported adrift near the Shambles light-vessel. Fortunately the weather was fine and a quick run was made to the scene, but it was found that a Greek steamship had taken the boats in tow. They were from the Belgian steamship *Alex van Opstal* which had sunk. The Greek steamer and her charges were escorted to a safe anchorage. Less than a month later, just before midnight on October 7th, the lifeboat was again launched to a ship torpedoed or mined near the light-vessel. Arriving on the scene in forty minutes they found the Dutch steamship *Binnendijk*, a large freighter bound from New York for Rotterdam, in a sinking state, but her crew of 41 had already been rescued by a naval examination vessel. The lifeboat was asked to stand by in case salvage should be attempted, but the steamship sank in a few hours. Arriving back at Weymouth they had to go out again half an hour later to investigate a heavy explosion in the area they had just left. Despite a wide search they could find nothing but unidentifiable wreckage. Just a week later they were back in the same area following a report of signal guns and rockets from the light-vessel herself. Going off at 10 in the evening of October 14th, in a strong easterly wind and moderate sea, they found that the light-vessel's boat had been manned by four of her own men and in spite of the darkness, wind and rain, had successfully saved the four man crew of an aeroplane which came down in the sea two miles away. This was an outstandingly courageous rescue which showed the wonderful spirit of the Trinity House men. At the best of times they were sitting targets for enemy aircraft and submarines, and it required a great degree of steadfastness to survive the stresses inevitably imposed. When the lifeboat arrived, the boat's crew were putting the rescued men on board a destroyer, but as their boat was by then water-logged the lifeboat coxswain took out the four rowers and returned them with their boat to the light-vessel.

On June 13th 1940, the steam tanker *British Inventor* was mined five miles off St. Alban's Head and in a calm sea she drifted south-westerly towards the Shambles. The Coastguard informed the lifeboat secretary and the lifeboat went out soon after eight in the morning. She found that an armed yacht had already taken off 25 of the crew including some injured, but a little later she was asked to take off the master and officers numbering fifteen. They then remained in attendance while Admiralty tugs attempted to tow the tanker to harbour, but she foundered in the early afternoon.

In the following month enemy air attacks increased greatly. On July 4th, the anti-aircraft ship *Foyle Bank* was bombed and sunk at Portland. At 8.15 in the morning of the 11th, the lifeboat authorities were told that an air battle was imminent and the crew assembled to stand by. Almost immediately they were told an armed yacht had been bombed ten miles south-east of Grove Point. This was the *Warrior II*, a steam yacht of over 1,000 tons, and she had sunk. While the lifeboat was searching for survivors, spent bullets and shrapnel were raining down but miraculously nobody was hit. Later a message came that an aircraft had been shot down ten miles south-east of the Bill, but again nothing could be found. Then a German aircraft came down within yards of the lifeboat and they rescued one of the crew, the rest having sunk with the plane. They got back at 1.30 in the afternoon, exhausted after many hours of cruising and straining to keep observation for any object that might support life. On the next day there was another long abortive search for aircraft reported in the sea.

On the 29th July the destroyer *Diligent* was bombed and sunk off Portland. Then on August 1st it was decided that the Shambles light-vessel, very much in the front line, should no longer be manned. As the weather was too bad for any available naval vessel to go alongside, the use of the lifeboat was requested to evacuate the seven men and their gear. The *Ryland* being away for an overhaul this service was carried out by the reserve boat *Queen Victoria*, a 51-feet Barnett type which had been at St. Peter Port, Guernsey, but was at Cowes being overhauled when the Channel Islands were occupied by the enemy. She was still on station on August 11th when there was another fruitless search after an air battle, followed by a further day-long search on the 13th. On the latter occasion, following up reports received from the

Coastguard, she first went east to White Nothe, returned and then made a second trip to Osmington Mills, and finally in the afternoon was called round the Bill to West Bay where two German aircraft had been shot down. She found no survivors or bodies but brought back pieces of wreckage for identification purposes—an important facet of the job in wartime. The crew had been on duty 12½ hours and at sea rather more than half this time. Another search on the 25th, when there was a great air battle and many enemy aircraft were brought down, ended this particular series of alarms.

On September 3rd 1941, three Admiralty trawlers were reported ashore between St. Alban's Head and Durdle Door. In spite of dense fog the Swanage lifeboat attended the *Olvina*, at St. Alban's Head, and the Weymouth lifeboat found the *Ceresio* firmly on the rocks at St. Oswald's Bay. At daylight, when the tide was making, the *Ceresio*'s head was towed round as she pivoted on a rock and a little later the tide floated her clear. Sturdy Arctic Ocean trawler as she was, she suffered little damage.

On June 6th 1944, Portland fishermen saved some airmen returning from bombing in support of the invasion of France. Although the lifeboat went out to join the small craft no more survivors were found after a long search. The last wartime service launch came on October 13th 1944, and proved to be a tragic affair. Late in the afternoon the American tank landing craft *LC(T)A.2454*, manned by Royal Navy men, got into difficulties off the Chesil Beach in a heavy south-westerly gale with rough seas. An Admiralty tug, on its way to help, found the going so hazardous that she could not round the Bill in the face of the gale and confused seas. The *Ryland* reached the scene, however, punching her way round 'like a half-tide rock'. Preparing to go alongside the craft, which was now ashore, she was almost in position when the naval authorities ashore signalled her to stand off again. The lifeboatmen were not to know why, but it transpired later that the order had been given because it was thought that in those conditions the lifeboat would surely be wrecked. The Coastguard had brought their rocket apparatus to the scene and by this means saved some lives, but the apparatus itself was swept into the sea by a huge wave which also took to their deaths the Inspecting Commander (Commander J. P. Penington-Legh, D.S.C., R.N.) and Coastguard R. H. Treadwell. Nine of the landing craft's crew were lost out of about twelve.

The first peacetime service came on November 1st 1945, when the lifeboat *Hearts of Oak* was on temporary duty at Weymouth. At about eight in the evening they were asked to launch to help the large Swedish tanker *Ariston*, which had a cargo of furnace oil from Trinidad for the Navy at Portland. She was so deeply laden with some 15,000 tons—a large cargo in those days—that she had grounded on a western outlier of the Shambles Bank. While strenuous efforts were made to get her clear by dockyard and other tugs the lifeboat stood by for twelve hours. She then had to return for fuel, but went out again almost at once. Fortunately the weather was calm and a smaller tanker, the *Chant 44*, was able to take out part of the *Ariston*'s cargo. Other tankers stood by, but she floated clear on the afternoon of the 2nd with help from the powerful tugs *Pilot*, *Thames* and *Storm King*.

It will be seen from the service records that many of the subsequent services were to pleasure craft, Weymouth being one of the principal centres in the yachting 'boom'. Here and there, however, are services to naval and commercial vessels, and a number of those to yachts have been difficult and dangerous in the extreme. On December 22nd 1946, the Naval landing craft *LC.723* was saved just as she was about to go ashore at White Nothe. She proved a difficult and unwieldy tow but was safely brought back to Portland. The service on January 12th 1947, to the Dutch motor vessel *Elisabeth*, took the lifeboat farther east than usual, for the timber-laden coaster was found at anchor with her motor broken down three miles off Chapman's Pool. She was towed back to Weymouth.

Of the pleasure craft services, the *Tarka* had her propeller fouled by lines from lobster pots; the *Glebe*'s crew were ashore birdsnesting under unscaleable cliffs when their dinghy broke adrift; the *Mallard*, a small boat with an 80-year-old lone fisherman, was found two miles south of the Shambles. These were more or less routine, but on June 6th 1948, there was an outstanding service for which Coxswain Frederick Palmer was awarded the bronze medal of the R.N.L.I. A converted naval motor launch, the yacht *Mite*, was on passage from Malta for London but her engine broke down when she was about fifteen miles west of Portland Bill. A wind from the S.S.W. was gradually increasing and the sea was rising, giving every prospect of really bad weather. To crown her misfortunes the yacht's radio failed. When they were closer to the shore and the cliffs were visible through the driving rain, two of her crew volunteered to take the dinghy ashore and summon help. It was a desperate thing to do considering the rocky nature of the coast, but they were in desperate straits. Fortunately the Coastguards spotted the tiny craft as it was driven shorewards and by signals indicated a safe landing place. Their message was at once phoned to the lifeboat secretary and the *Ryland* was on her way in five minutes, but it took nearly three hours, ploughing into the teeth of the gale, to reach the *Mite*. She was now precariously anchored off the Bill. The owner would not abandon his craft and asked for a tow. Although the weather was worsening the Coxswain agreed and began by heading south and then turning east to give a wide berth to the Race and the Shambles Bank. Several times the yacht sheered wildly, her steering gear not working properly, and twice the tow-rope parted, and was reconnected. Then there was a third break and the weather was by then so bad the Coxswain decided it was too dangerous to tow any longer. They were within two miles of the shore—dangerously close in the circumstances, and visibility was very poor. Going alongside the yacht, both vessels tossing wildly, the three men were taken off, but their baggage was washed away. Then they made for Weymouth and arrived half an hour after midnight, the lifeboat's struggle with the elements having lasted eleven hours. The yacht was later washed up at Ringstead.

Not a year later Coxswain Palmer added a silver medal to his bronze and Mechanic MacDermott was awarded a bronze for a hazardous service off Chesil Beach. On the evening of April 2nd 1949, a small steam tug, the *HS.161*, which had been working at Devonport Dockyard, but had been bought by a London man, was steaming across Lyme Bay. There was a strong south-west wind with heavy seas and drifting banks of fog. The tug had been laid up for a time and was possibly not in very good condition for her boilers began to give trouble. Losing steering way, they finally became lost in the very poor visibility, blowing the whistle for help. The Coastguard heard the whistle and summoned the lifeboat. As she set out he was able to tell the coxswain by radio-telephone that the tug was now a mile and a half north-west of the Bill and drifting into West Bay. Later, having rounded the Bill and forged northwards for a while, the lifeboatmen caught a glimpse of her, but lost her again in the fog. Keeping in close radio touch with the Coastguard headquarters and with the rescue apparatus team waiting on Chesil Beach, there followed half an hour of searching and occasional sightings. Eventually this grim hide and seek was over when they got close to the tug, now broadside to the beach and not more than fifty yards away. The owner had intended to beach her, but that would have been suicidal in the seas which were sweeping in from the south, and the Coastguards on shore signalled to her to keep off. As the lifeboat drew alongside it was realised that most of the tug's four-man crew were in a dazed state and apparently under the impression they would be able to walk ashore in a short while. There being no time to discuss the issue, a rope was thrown to the one man on board who seemed to be aware of the true situation, and it was made fast. Within seconds the lifeboat had the tug in tow and they were fighting to get away from the surf, so close had they come to the beach. Then followed a hard slog of two hours back to Weymouth.

Most of the later services of the *Ryland* were to pleasure craft and the details would be somewhat repetitious. Of commercial vessels, the Belgian *Francine*, sheltering while bound from Shoreham for Fowey, on December 18th 1951, went adrift in Weymouth Bay while her master was ashore purchasing stores. There was a whole southerly gale and very rough sea when the understandably agitated Captain van den Buelcki asked the lifeboat Coxswain to put him back on his ship. This was speedily done. Luckily the *Francine* was able to get under weigh again and with the lifeboat standing by return to the sheltering arms of Portland Harbour. The Dutch motor vessel *Heemskerk*, on December 3rd 1953, while bound from Par for Gluckstadt with china clay, suddenly began to leak aft. She was well out in the Channel and the situation was desperate. Her signal was relayed by the Shambles lightvessel and the lifeboat came out to escort her to Weymouth. A lifeboatman was put on board as a pilot and the fastest possible speed was made, but by the time they reached harbour the coaster's stern was awash.

A third commercial vessel assisted in this period was another Dutch motor coaster, the *Pegasus*, which was on passage from Ellesmere Port for Rotterdam on December 30th 1956, when her deck cargo began to explode. This consisted of drums of calcium carbide and sodium which the crew at great risk attempted to throw overboard. When the trouble started they were 25 miles south-west of Portland Bill and a long-drawn battle began. The weather was bad with a strong south-westerly gale, heavy rain squalls and a rough sea. At four in the afternoon it was already so dark that a Shackleton aircraft dropped flares to show the position of the casualty. The flames flared spasmodicallly as the *Pegasus* made all speed towards Portland, and other ships, in the true spirit of the sea, altered course to be at hand if she had to be abandoned. Her gallant and persevering crew gradually got the fire under control, and while the frigate H.M.S. *Tumult* played hoses on her deck, the Weymouth lifeboat made fast alongside and a naval fire-float arrived from Portland dockyard. Sparks and flames could be seen for some time after she was anchored off the harbour, but fortunately the fire did not get a grip on the cargo below decks, and surprisingly little structural damage resulted.

An unusual service was to the Dutch submarine *Tijgerhaai* on October 19th 1955. She touched ground in Weymouth Bay at about four in the morning in a south-easterly gale and rough sea. Fortunately the tide was rising and, using her engines to prevent herself going farther inshore, she floated again at about 6.30. The lifeboat *Edmund and Mary Robinson*, on temporary duty at the station, escorted her to moorings in Portland harbour.

During her service at Weymouth from 1930 to 1957, the *William and Clara Ryland*, and the various relief boats during her periodic overhauls, made no less than 181 launches and rescued 149 persons, besides many others landed or towed to land in their own craft. Of this total 22 were saved in the war years. Of the 86 successful services, 51 were to pleasure craft, 18 to commercial craft, five to fishing vessels, six to naval vessels, two to aircraft and four miscellaneous, such as swimmers and cliff climbers. No less than 105 of the lives actually saved were those of yachtsmen, and probably some of those classed as fishermen should be added to this total. However, the inescapable conclusion is that pleasure boat casualties account for a very large proportion of the calls on Weymouth station, a situation which prevails to this day and, also, of course, at many other stations. Weymouth is naturally a popular venue both for local yachts and for yachts on passage. One hopes the yachting fraternity subscribes gladly to R.N.L.I. funds.

The new Weymouth lifeboat arrived in November 1957, a 52-feet Barnett-type, the largest and most advanced in production at that time. She was built from the bequest of Doctor Locke, of Tunbridge Wells, and was named *Frank Spiller Locke* at a ceremony on June 14th 1958, by his great-niece Miss Helen Harries.

The vagaries of the demand for life-saving services are well shown by the record of the years 1958-60, in each of which there were only one or two services, whereas in 1956 there had been six, in 1957 and also in 1961 eight, and in 1962 twelve, a number not to be surpassed until 1968 with fourteen. The *Frank Spiller Locke*'s first service came on October 31st 1958, when the Coastguard reported a motor yacht broken down three miles south-west of Portland, with the frigate H.M.S. *Murray* standing by in case the yacht had to be abandoned. The lifeboat found the casualty to be the *Sevona*, of Gloucester, and was able to tow her back to Weymouth.

The service on July 12th 1959, was to an unusual type of yacht—the Dutch barge yacht *Scaldis V.*, belonging to Cowes and bound from Falmouth for Gosport. She was in distress a mile and a half south-south-east of the Bill, with her motor broken down, her rudder damaged, and leaking badly. Seven persons and a dog were on board. She too was towed back to safety at Weymouth.

An outstanding service which earned the formal Thanks inscribed on vellum for Coxswain Frederick Palmer was that on the evening of January 1st 1961. The small motor vessel *Vectis Isle*, of Cowes, in ballast, had been sheltering from a south-westerly gale in Weymouth Bay when she dragged her anchors and eventually grounded on Portland Breakwater. It was a very dark night, with rain, and a strong south-easterly swell was breaking right over the breakwater and the stranded vessel. The lifeboat found her pounding heavily on the pell-mell concrete blocks and in imminent danger of being holed and sunk. The Coxswain decided to try to tow her off and, having anchored, they veered down towards her. A line was then sent over her by means of the line-gun, followed by a towing wire which was made fast. Going slowly ahead the lifeboat got the line taut, at the same time heaving on her anchor cable. After a few minutes the *Vectis Isle* began to turn in the right direction and the Coxswain signalled to her master to heave on his own anchor. Thus by their joint efforts she came clear and they made for the north entrance. However, the dead weight of the tow and adverse tidal currents proved too much for that course and the Coxswain had to heave-to near the eastern entrance, allowing the wind, on their beam, to take both of them through to the open sea. It was a triumph of manoeuvre and seamanship, making use of the elements to the fullest degree. Once outside, the tow to Weymouth harbour was slow but straightforward.

A service which began at eight in the morning of October 4th 1961, led to a long search and finally the safe mooring of the cabin cruiser *Paulina* at Poole—possibly the longest service run undertaken by any Weymouth lifeboat. It so happened the reserve lifeboat *Lloyd's* was on station at the time. The yacht, with four on board, first radioed for help when she was five miles south of the Bill and had suffered an engine breakdown. There was a gale from the S.S.E. which whipped up a very rough sea, and the conditions were such that the navy thought it advisable to send out the frigate *Berwick* and a helicopter. In response to broadcast 'Mayday' calls, the British coaster *Pladda* and the German tanker *Michael M.* also joined in the search, but it was the Irish motor vessel *City of Waterford* which eventually found the yacht and first got a line on board. They began to tow eastwards and after getting into radio touch with the lifeboat, met about five miles south of St. Alban's Head an hour later. Then followed a five hours tow to Poole.

Nine young Sea Cadets and their officers were saved on the evening of August 23rd 1962. The auxiliary schooner *Garland*, on a cruise from Cowes, was driven into West Bay by a south-westerly gale. When they were half a mile off Chesil Beach at Abbotsbury they burnt flares which were seen at once and reported to the Coastguard. The *Frank Spiller Locke* was away within seven minutes of the call. Having rounded the Bill they found that the *Garland* had been able to get away from the shore by a combination of her motor and skilful sailing. She was slowly but surely heading south-eastwards to the open channel. The lifeboat escorted her until, having rounded the Bill, the schooner's drogue rope unfortunately fouled her propeller, stopping the motor. The lifeboat then took her in tow for Weymouth.

A service on April 12th 1963, to a type of craft now rarely seen, the clipper-bowed steam yacht *Medea*, built in 1904, resulted in saving this graceful survivor of the past. Her compound steam engines broke down when she was seven miles west of the Bill. A fresh south-westerly breeze and moderate sea was tending to take her into the dangerous waters of West Bay, so the lifeboat was called out at once, met her an hour and a half later and towed her to Weymouth.

The Inshore Rescue Service was called upon on May 15th 1965, when the motor boat *The Poo* broke down between Portland and Weymouth in a light breeze and slight sea. The local motor boat *Eileen* put out to tow in the casualty and was, in fact, so doing when it was decided that as the tide was against them they might need additional help. Accordingly the lifeboat went out and escorted them to Weymouth.

A personal act of bravery marked the next service a fortnight later, on May 29th 1965. Early in the afternoon it was reported that the yacht *Dehra* had grounded north of the pier and as she was quite close at hand, Coxswain Pavey with two lifeboatmen went out in his boat to see if they could help. There was a moderate north-easterly wind and choppy sea, and they found the yacht firmly aground with the waves sending spray over her. It was low tide and the water too shallow for getting alongside to help at that time, so they returned to harbour. It was decided to send out the lifeboat as she could stand by and use her line-throwing gun if it was necessary to take off the yacht's crew. Arriving back on the scene in a short while the Coxswain was faced with the problem of finding a channel by which he could get as close to the casualty as possible. Anchoring, they veered down on the cable, but the swell and the shallow water made the manoeuvre difficult. Then they fouled a marker buoy, one of a pair which had been laid down for a yacht race, and had to draw back to their anchor and try another spot. This time, by manoeuvring at speed they avoided the buoys and got within a hundred yards of the *Dehra* where they were occasionally touching bottom in the troughs of the swells. Four rocket lines were fired, but the two which fell across the yacht were fumbled by her crew. The Coxswain judged it imperative to get a line across as when the tide turned, with the swell, this could throw the yacht over on her beam ends. One of the lifeboatmen, Donald Laker, a strong swimmer, volunteered to take a line across and, having stripped off his outer clothing, plunged into the surf. After a few anxious minutes he scrambled on board the *Dehra* and a tow line was quickly pulled across by means of the line he had carried. They had barely secured the rope when a heavy swell caused the yacht to lurch violently. The yacht's owner was thrown across the deck and against an iron stanchion, badly cutting his head. The others were severely bruised, but Donald Laker at once began first aid. They carried the owner below and a watcher on the pier, seeing this through powerful binoculars, reported to the Coastguard that there was an injured person on board. A helicopter was called but meanwhile Dr. Gordon Wallace, the station's honorary medical adviser, asked a friend to take him out to the yacht or if that proved impossible to the lifeboat. While this was going on the lifeboat had been able to tow the yacht's head around so that she faced the swell and rode more easily. The wind also dropped. Mr. E. A. Hall, skilfully handling his 'Boston whaler' managed to put the doctor on the yacht and to return Donald Laker to the lifeboat. By the time the helicopter arrived the doctor had appraised the situation and decided that it was inadvisable to move his patient at that time. After an hour or so the tide rose sufficiently to refloat the yacht and she was towed back to harbour. Donald Laker was awarded the R.N.L.I. bronze medal, and the formal Thanks went to the crew as a whole.

A lengthy search which eventually took them far out into the English Channel was mounted on May 29th 1966, when a small yacht of the 'folk-boat' class, the *Huckleberry Finn*, was reported dismasted and adrift with her motor broken down. Her sole occupant had spoken to passing vessels asking them to radio for someone to tow him to Portland. The lifeboat went off about nine in the evening in a strong easterly wind and rough sea, but although other vessels were helping, and after daybreak a helicopter also, no trace could be found of the yacht. The lifeboat had to return for fuel after 17 hours at sea and then the reports seemed hopeless. However, at six in the evening of the 30th they received a further Coastguard report that a yacht, probably a folk-boat, had been seen by a helicopter pilot about twenty miles S.S.W. of Portland Bill, considerably west of the original reported position. They had lowered to the lone yachtsman a Very pistol so that he could send up a flare at intervals. Going out again, the lifeboat was searching all night, but in spite of their radar were still unable to locate the yacht. In the early morning the frigate H.M.S. *Malcolm* joined the search and her mast-head observers, with a far greater range of vision, located the *Huckleberry Finn* at about half past six in the morning. She took the yacht in tow and handed her over to the lifeboat about seventeen miles off the Bill. They arrived back at Weymouth soon after eleven after searches totalling nearly 35 hours.

There was another outstanding service in the early hours of January 24th 1967, when two people were saved from the catamaran *Ranger of Essex* which was on passage from Jersey. Flares had been reported off Portland Bill while a wind from the W.S.W. with heavy squalls was blowing against the tide and making very unpleasant conditions for any small craft. The lifeboat reached the scene in an hour, and after twenty minutes of manoeuvring had the 'cat' in tow. The frigate H.M.S. *Whitby* arrived at about the same time and stood by in case of need. In the prevailing conditions and darkness Coxswain Pavey decided not to take the narrow inshore passage but to go southabout round the Race and the Shambles Bank. The towrope broke, but was reconnected, and the disabled yacht was safely brought to Weymouth harbour at 5.30 in the morning.

The station doctor, who had played his part in several earlier rescues, was awarded the formal Thanks of the R.N.L.I. for his part in a service on June 19th 1967. At about three in the afternoon a radio report was received that the Russian diesel-electric vessel *Viktor Lyagin* had picked up the British sloop-yacht *Bilberry* with three on board, one of whom was dead and the other two ill. She was then fifteen miles south-east of the Bill. The lifeboat went out twenty minutes later with Dr. Gordon Wallace on board. The sea was smooth but visibility poor through mist. The Russian vessel was moving slowly towards them, but before they met, the Royal Navy patrol launch *P.1114* came alongside to ask if she could help. She drew away at high speed with the usual panache and the lifeboat was drawn by her wash into contact with her port quarter, causing damage to the 'bow pudding'. Soon afterwards came a radio request that a helicopter should take the doctor to an inflatable dinghy which had been put overboard from the patrol launch so that he could board the yacht more quickly. This was done after several anxious moments when the helicopter's winch jammed with an airman and the doctor suspended over the sea. Eventually the trouble was rectified and the doctor lowered to the yacht. Having examined the men he considered it inadvisable to move the one who was most seriously ill and accordingly remained with him while the yacht was taken in tow for Weymouth.

There have been many later services, almost all to yachts of various sizes and rigs. In most cases they have been safely towed home and their amateur crews thankfully landed on *terra firma*. There was a touch of humour about one case where two gallants left their ladies on board their small craft anchored off Chesil Cove while they came ashore in the dinghy for a can of petrol. The wind and the sea were rising and a short while later they found themselves unable to return to the yacht. The situation could have been tragic but for the lifeboat. The ladies had a nerve-wracking couple of hours while she came round the Bill to their rescue.

BOAT RECORD, PORTLAND AND WEYMOUTH

Years on Station	Length, Breadth, Oars/Crew	Type, Weight, Cost	Year built, (Off. No.) Builder	Boat's Name, Donor, Authority
(a) at Portland				
1826- c. 1850	20' 6' 9" 6/7	Plenty 1t5 £100	1825 Plenty, Newbury	(no name) Local subscriptions R.N.I.P.L.S. (Dorset Branch Ass'n)
(b) at Weymouth				
1869- 1887	33' 8' 6" 10/12	SR 2t10 £276	1869 Forrestt, Limehouse	*Agnes Harriet* Earl of Strafford R.N.L.I.
1887- 1903	34' 8' 10/13	SR 3t12 £347	1887 (141) Hansen, Cowes	*Friern Watch* E. Homan, Finchley R.N.L.I.
1903- 1924	38' 9' 4" 12/15	W 6t £1023	1903 (513) Thames Iron Works, Blackwall	*Friern Watch* as above R.N.L.I.
1924- 1929	40' 11' -/8	W(M) 10t5 £7156	1918 (651)[1] Saunders,[2] E. Cowes	*Samuel Oakes* Legacy Mrs. E. M. Laing, R.N.L.I.

1929-	40' 6"	W(M)	1929 (721)	*Lady Kylsant*
1930	11' 8"	12t	S. J. White,	Royal Mail and Union
	-/8	£5865	Cowes	R.N.L.I. [Castle S.S.Co.
1930-	51'	B(M)	1930 (735)	*William and Clara Ryland*
1957	13' 6"	26t13	Saunders-Roe	Legacy Wm. Ryland,
	-/8	£9413	Cowes	R.N.L.I. [Sheffield
1957-	52'	B(M)	1957 (939)	*Frank Spiller Locke*
	14'	27t19	Groves and	Legacy Dr. F. S. Locke,
	-/7	£38500	Guttridge,	R.N.L.I. [Tunbridge Wells
			Cowes	

1 Previously stationed at Spurn Point, Yorkshire.
2 Begun by Summers and Payne, completed by Saunders.

SERVICE RECORD, WEYMOUTH

Agnes Harriet Lifeboat
1887 Nov.   1   Brigantine *Maren*, of Fano (Denmark), saved   7

Friern Watch Lifeboat
1888 Nov.   25   Schooner *Mary Davies*, of Aberystwyth, saved   3

Friern Watch (second) Lifeboat
1904 Feb.   26   Ship *Alanda*, of Hamburg, stood by
1905 Feb.   26   Barque *County of Anglesea*, of Liverpool, gave help and
                                                              saved   2
1914 Dec.   11   Schooner *Ardente*, of Paimpol (France), saved   5
1916 Nov.   18   Barque *Gladys*, of Bristol, landed 20
                  Barque *Celticburn*, of Greenock, landed 28
                      do.   (second service), reboarded crew

Charles Deere James reserve Lifeboat
1920 Oct.   5   Tender to H.M.S. *Warspite*, stood by and escorted to
                                                              Portland
Friern Watch (second) Lifeboat
1921 Sept.   18   Spritsail barge *Cecilia*, of London, assisted to save
                                                       barge and   7
1922 Apr.   1   Spritsail barge *Savoy*, of Dover, stood by
        Dec.   21   Schooner *Meta*, of Troense (Denmark), saved   7
1923 Feb.   23   Steamship *Cragside*, of Newcastle, landed 10
                  Ketch *Phoenix*, of Plymouth, landed 2
1924 Jan.   12   Schooner *Fanny Crossfield*, of Barrow, stood by

Samuel Oakes Lifeboat
1925 Jan.   1   Brigantine *La Servannaise*, of St. Malo, stood by
               2   do.   (second service), stood by
        Apr.   3   Yacht *Rosenn*, of Southampton, assisted to refloat yacht
        Sept. 22   Schooner *Duchess*, of Chester, saved   4
              23   do.   reboarded crew
1926 Aug.   27   Motor yacht *Bonita*, of Teignmouth, towed in yacht and 3
        Nov.   19   Motor boat *Rose Mary*, of Weymouth, saved boat and   3
1928 Feb.   16   Barge *Emma*, of Weymouth, stood by and escorted
                                                       to Portland
        May   18   Motor yacht *Valetta*, of Falmouth, stood by
        June 26   Cutter *Bonnie Jean*, of Poole, saved cutter and   2

The s.s. Gertrude, *of West Hartlepool, bound for Rotterdam from Huelva, struck Blacknor Point on August 26th 1894 and was wrecked.*

[*Photo: Eric Latcham Collection*]

The Milford ketch Verbena *was bound from South Wales for Weymouth with culm when she struck the west side of Portland Bill on July 22nd 1903.*

[*Photo: Eric Latcham Collection*]

The German steamship Okahandja, *homeward bound with iron ore from Spain, drove on the Tor Rock, Portland, in dense fog on June 8th 1910. She was refloated the next day after some cargo had been jettisoned.* [*Photo: Eric Latcham Collection*]

By coincidence, another steamship laden with iron ore was wrecked in this locality on March 25th 1912—the s.s. Myrtledene, *wrecked at Mutton Cove, Portland whilst* en route *for Rotterdam.* [*Photo: Eric Latcham Collection*]

Lady Kylsant Lifeboat

1929	Aug.	26	Steamship *Jolly Esmond*, of London, stood by and gave help	
1930	Jan.	12	Steamship *Forester*, of Cardiff, saved	7
	Sept.	19	Ketch *Leonie*, of St. Malo, saved	2
		20	do. saved vessel	

William and Clara Ryland Lifeboat

1932	Sept.	8	Yacht *Hope*, of Weymouth, saved vessel and	4
	Nov.	11	Lifeboat *Thomas Masterman Hardy*, of Lyme Regis, gave help	
1933	Feb.	25	Steamship *Engineer*, of Newcastle, stood by until taken in tow	
	July	31	Yacht *Heron*, of Dublin, saved vessel and	4
1934	Mar.	19	Steam trawler *La Violette*, of Ostend, towed vessel to Weymouth	
	May	2	Motor vessel *Westlaan*, of Groningen (Netherlands), stood by and assisted vessel to safety	
	Oct.	3	Motor yawl yacht *Lavinia*, of London, saved yacht and	2
1935	Mar.	9	Barge *Shamrock*, of Faversham, stood by and refloated barge	
	Apr.	7	Motor boat *Seafarer*, of Weymouth, saved boat and	4
1936	Feb.	16	Motor vessel *Winchester Castle*, of London, stood by	

The Brothers (reserve) Lifeboat

	May	29	Motor yacht *Little Mariner*, of London, saved yacht

William and Clara Ryland Lifeboat

	Oct.	31	Fishing boat, of Weymouth, saved boat and	1
	Nov.	12	Boat of H.M.S. *Lucia*, landed 4 men from breakwater	
1937	Feb.	25	Motor vessel *Gertruda*, of London, gave help	
	Aug.	18	Auxiliary yacht *Spray*, of Poole, saved yacht and	7

Alfred and Clara Heath (reserve) Lifeboat

1938	Aug.	4	Auxiliary yacht *Gisèle Aimée*, of St. Malo, assisted to save yacht and	3

William and Clara Ryland Lifeboat

	Nov.	26	Steamship *Panachrandos*, of Andros, escorted vessel to anchorage	
1939	Feb.	12	A rowing boat, saved	2
	Aug.	16	Motor yacht *Jane*, of Poole, gave help	
	Sept.	15	Boats of steamship *Alex Van Opstal*, of Antwerp, stood by	
	Oct.	7	Steamship *Binnendijk*, of Rotterdam, stood by	
		14	Boat of *Shambles* Light-vessel, saved	4
	Nov.	22	Steamship *Elena R.*, of Syra (Greece), landed 24 from Shambles Light-vessel	
1940	Jan	1	Steamship *Neti*, of Susak (Yugoslavia), stood by	
		2	do. (second launch), stood by	
	Apr.	22	Motor boat *Edith May*, of Weymouth, saved boat and	2
	June	13	Steam tanker *British Inventor*, of London, saved two boats and	15
	July	11	German aircraft, saved	1

Queen Victoria (reserve) Lifeboat

	Aug.	1	*Shambles* Light-vessel, landed 7 and gear
		13	German aircraft, salved wreckage

William and Clara Ryland Lifeboat

1941	Apr.	23	H.M. Hired Drifter *Dol-Fyn*, gave help
	Sept.	3	H.M. Minesweeper *Ceresio*, saved vessel

Hearts of Oak (reserve) Lifeboat

1945	Nov.	1	Motor tanker *Ariston*, of Gothenburg, stood by
1946	July	14	Motor boat *Zamaya*, of Dartmouth, towed in boat and 2

William and Clara Ryland Lifeboat

	Sept.	20	Motor boat *O. B. Joyfull*, of Weymouth ⎫ saved boats	
			Fishing boat, of Weymouth ⎭ and	3
	Dec.	22	H.M. Landing Craft *LC.723*, saved craft and	11
1947	Jan.	12	Motor vessel *Elisabeth*, of Rotterdam, saved vessel and	5
	Apr.	5	Yacht *Kittiwake*, saved yacht and	1
			Motor fishing boat *Pam*, saved boat and	2
	June	18	Motor fishing vessel *Eliane Thérèse*, of Boulogne, towed in trawler and 8	
	Sept.	26	Motor boat *Tarka*, saved boat and	2
1948	Apr.	7	Yacht *Glebe*, of Weymouth, saved yacht and	2
			Dinghy, saved dinghy	
	May	14	Motor boat *Mallard*, of Weymouth, saved boat and	1
	June	6	Motor yacht *Mite*, of London, saved	3
	July	26	Motor yacht *Dinah*, towed yacht and 4 to harbour	

Hearts of Oak (reserve) Lifeboat

1948	Aug.	8	Motor yacht *Paviroma*, of Southampton, saved yacht and	5
	Oct.	2	Yacht *Glebe*, of Weymouth, saved yacht and	1

William and Clara Ryland Lifeboat

1949	Mar.	27	Motor yacht *Puffin III*, of Weymouth, saved yacht and	2
		28	Motor boat *Robin II*, of Bridport, saved boat	
		29	Drifter attached to H.M.S. *King George V*, refloated drifter	
	Apr.	2	Ex-naval tug *HS,161*. saved tug and	4

John and Mary Meiklam of Gladswood (reserve) Lifeboat

	Sept.	4	Man over the cliff at White Nothe, landed injured man
		5	Motor yacht *Lilida*, of Southampton, saved yacht and	3

William and Clara Ryland Lifeboat

		8	Motor yacht *Juliette*, of Falmouth, saved yacht and	3
		15	Sailing boat *Brigand*, saved boat and	2
1951	Apr.	3	Motor cruiser *Paddy Moya*, of Christchurch, saved yacht and	2
	May	6	Ketch yacht *Fortis*, of Portsmouth, saved yacht and	2
	Nov.	30	Auxiliary yacht *Penguin*, towed in yacht and 4	
	Dec.	28	Motor vessel *Francine*, of Antwerp, boarded master and escorted vessel to harbour	
1952	Apr.	17	Motor yacht *Coila*, of Plymouth, towed in yacht and 2	
	July	27	Dinghy, salved dinghy	
	Aug.	2	Cutter yacht *Idler*, of Southampton, saved yacht and	1
		18	Cabin cruiser *Diana II*, of London, saved yacht and	4
	Sept.	5	Yacht *Joananna*, saved yacht and	3

Milburn (reserve) Lifeboat

1953	Apr.	4	Cutter yacht *Lalla Rookh*, of Beaumaris, escorted yacht and 5 to harbour

William and Clara Ryland Lifeboat

	Dec.	3	Motor vessel *Heemskerk*, of Rotterdam, supplied pilot and escorted to harbour

Milburn reserve Lifeboat

1954	July	17	Yacht *Yana*, saved yacht and	2
	Sept.	8	Sailing dinghy, saved dinghy	

William and Clara Ryland Lifeboat
   20 Trawler *Flower of the Fleet*, of Brixham, towed in vessel and 2
1955 Oct. 6 Cutter yacht *Raider*, of Cardiff, saved yacht and   1

Edmund and Mary Robinson reserve Lifeboat
   19 Royal Netherlands Navy submarine *Tijgerhaai*, stood
      by and escorted to Portland

William and Clara Ryland Lifeboat
1956 July 20 Yacht *Midnight*, towed yacht to harbour
  Aug.   1 Yacht *Marjealine*, of Le Havre, saved yacht and   4
     21 Yacht *Mary Rose*, of Brixham, towed in yacht and 3
  Sept. 1 Fishing boat *June*, saved boat and   2
       Yacht *Capella*, of Portsmouth, saved yacht and 10
  Dec. 30 Motor vessel *Pegasus*, of Groningen (Netherlands),
      escorted vessel
1957 Jan.   3 Motor boat *Maria*, of Weymouth, saved boat and   1
  June   4 Yacht *Solent Gipsy*, towed in yacht and 3
  July 12 Yacht *Gay Nixie*, of Lymington, saved yacht and   1
     17 Schooner yacht *Olivia*, of Plymouth, saved yacht and 7
  Aug. 11 Yacht *Inschallah*, of Hamburg, escorted yacht and 6 to
      harbour
       Yacht *Maze*, of Rotterdam, escorted yacht and 5 to harbour
     20 Yacht *Rona*, saved yacht and   3
     24 Yacht *Tarifa*, saved yacht and   7

Frank Spiller Locke Lifeboat
1958 Oct. 31 Motor yacht *Sevona*, of Gloucester, saved yacht and 3
1959 July 12 Barge yacht *Scaldis V*, of Cowes, saved yacht (also a
      dog) and 7
1960 June   4 Rowing boat, of Weymouth, saved boat
  Nov.   4 Motor vessel *Lesrix*, of Hull, landed a body
1961 Jan.   1 Motor vessel *Vectis Isle*, of Cowes, saved vessel and 5
      6 Motor yacht *Nanyao*, of Southampton, landed 2 from
      steamship *Pavlos*, of Beirut
     27 Motor vessel *Tjoba*, of Groningen (Netherlands),
      escorted vessel
  May   6 Whaler from H.M.N.Z.S. *Taranaki*, recovered whaler

Lloyd's (reserve) Lifeboat
  Aug. 3-4 Yacht *Fylanna*, in tow of tanker *Esso Lyndhurst*, escorted
      vessels to Portland
     13 Fishing vessel *Our Jennie*, saved boat and   2
     15 Rowing boat *Feathers*, saved boat
  Oct.   6 Motor yacht *Paulina*, towed yacht and 4 to Poole

Frank Spiller Locke Lifeboat
1962 Apr. 23 Rowing boats *Mercury* and *Blue Peter*, of Weymouth,
      saved boats
  May 19 Outboard motor boat, saved boat and   2
  July   8 Swimmer, took him to his ship—H.M.S. *Rothesay*
     21 Yacht *Ituna*, of Dublin, saved yacht and   8
     24 Motor fishing vessel *Four Girls*, of Weymouth, towed
      boat and 2 to Lulworth
     31 Yacht *Themlyay*, of Hull, towed in yacht and 2
  Aug.   5 Sailing dinghy *Hilda Kate*, towed in dinghy and 2
     15 Boy missing on cliff at Durdle Door, gave help
     23 Training schooner *The Garland*, of Cowes, saved vessel and 10
  Sept. 5 Yacht *Fair Winds*, towed in yacht and 4

		29	Red flashing buoy adrift, towed buoy to Portland	
			Cabin cruiser *Medinia*, saved yacht and	2
1963	Mar.	10	Persons on the rocks at Lulworth Cove, landed a body	
	Apr.	12	Steam yacht *Medea*, of Colchester, towed yacht to harbour	
	Aug.	7	Motor yacht *Colley*, landed 4 from motor vessel	
			Zwijndrecht, of Rotterdam	
		18	Motor boat *Dolce Vita*, of Weymouth, saved boat and	4
	Sept.	18	Yacht *Calypso V*, of London, towed in yacht and 4	
1964	May	17	Cabin cruiser *Lorerelei*, of Weymouth, saved	2
	Sept.	6	Yacht *Laura*, saved yacht and	1
		9	Small boat, saved boat and	2

Lloyd's reserve Lifeboat
	Nov.	9	Motor vessel *Ramona*, of Harlingen (Netherlands), supplied	
			pilot and escorted to harbour	

Frank Spiller Locke Lifeboat
1965	May	15	Motor boat *The Poo*, in tow of motor boat *Eileen*,	
			escorted boats	
		16	Motor yacht *Whiffle*, escorted yacht	
			Speed-boat *Prince*, towed in boat	
1965	May	29	Yacht *Dehra*, of Guernsey, saved yacht and	5
	Aug.	29	Girl fallen over the cliff at West Nothe, landed a body	
	Sept.	8	Yacht *Gladeye*, in tow of Royal Fleet Auxiliary motor	
			tanker *Black Ranger*, escorted to Portland	
	Oct.	17	Dinghy, saved	1

Peter and Sarah Blake (reserve) Lifeboat
1966	May	1	Motor cruiser *Windy Wyne*, of Falmouth, saved yacht and	5

Frank Spiller Locke Lifeboat
		30	'Folkboat' yacht *Huckleberry Finn*, of Southampton,	
			towed in yacht and 1	
	Sept.	12	Yacht *Mignonette*, of Southampton, saved yacht and	2
	Dec.	9	Motor vessel *Alatyrles*, of Leningrad, took out a doctor and	
			landed a sick man, thereby saving a life	1
1967	Jan.	24	Catamaran *Ranger of Essex*, saved vessel and	2
	Mar.	26	Yacht *Wombat*, escorted yacht and 4 to harbour	

Lloyd's (reserve) Lifeboat
	Apr.	21	Motor fishing vessel *Tizer*, of Weymouth, saved vessel and	2

Frank Spiller Locke Lifeboat
	June	9	Canoe, helped police to recover canoe	
		19	Sloop yacht *Bilberry*, towed yacht and 2 to harbour,	
			landed a body	
	July	23	Motor yacht *Tonga*, towed in yacht and 3	
	Aug.	9	Yacht *Apeloiter*, saved yacht and	2
	Sept.	19	Dinghy, escorted dinghy	
	Oct.	14	'Seabat', saved craft and	1
1968	Apr.	30	Cabin cruiser *Dorset Maid*, saved yacht	
	June	5	Cabin cruiser *Cilla*, saved yacht and	1
		14	Sailing dinghy, saved dinghy	
		15	Yacht *Gnu*, saved yacht and	2
	July	13	Motor launch *Chindwyn V*, saved launch and	3
		19	Sloop yacht *Quest Levant*, saved yacht and	2
		29	Fishing boat *Four Girls*, of Weymouth, saved boat	
		31	Motor yacht *Keltisle II*, of London, saved yacht and	4
	Aug.	5	Yacht, towed in yacht and	1
		28	Yacht *Lady Loren*, saved yacht and	4

		31	Motor yacht *Robert Clive*, of Rochester, saved yacht	
	Sept.	2	Yacht *Frances Helen*, saved yacht and	5
		6	Cabin cruiser *Kantara*, saved yacht and	4
		23	Bermudian sloop *Uhuru*, landed 2	
		30	Yacht *Follette*, recovered a body	
1969	Jan.	12	Person in the sea, recovered clothing	
	Apr.	6	Yacht *Phan Khu*, of London, saved yacht and	5
	Aug.	1	Yacht *Chloe*, of London, in tow of motor vessel *Sand Lark*, gave help and landed 4	
		15	Trawler *Caprice des Mers*, of Dieppe, gave help to an injured man taken from the burning ketch yacht *Northward*	
	Oct.	25	Motor boat *Tap*, saved boat and	2
	Nov.	23	Motor vessel *Burja*, of Riga, landed a sick woman, thereby saving a life	1
1970	Jan.	4	Yacht *Dib II*, saved yacht and	2
	Mar.	11	Motor boat *Weyward*, saved boat and	2

3

KIMMERIDGE and CHAPMAN'S POOL

THE PILOT'S HANDBOOK said of St. Alban's Head, 'there is generally a race off the head, particularly in blowing weather, caused by the uneven ground. The overfalls extend a mile off shore.' Nevertheless, in former times sailing coasters were often tempted to come too close to the land in their efforts to dodge the tides, and vessels of all sizes came to grief in foggy weather. Today most of the traffic close to the headland consists of pleasure craft and it usually turns out to be a rougher passage than would have been experienced farther out.

The name St. Alban's is sometimes correctly rendered as St. Aldhelm's, after the first Bishop of Sherborne, appointed in the eighth century. A small chapel, about 32-feet square, with Norman features, is still to be seen on the 350-feet high summit of the headland. It is said to have been built in 1140 on the site of an earlier cell, by a father who had witnessed the tragedy of his daughter and her bridegroom being drowned nearby. A turret, still in place, probably supported a brazier in which a fire was shown to warn shipping.

Near the cliff path leading eastwards to Durlston Head, at oddly named East Man, is a small patch of level ground with the graves of some of the people washed ashore from the East Indiaman *Halsewell* in 1786. Others are buried in Worth Matravers churchyard. The sheer horror of this wreck prompted a very full account in the contemporary *Annual Register*, and half a century later Charles Dickens used the story in his novel *The Long Journey*. The *Halsewell*, 758 tons, a large ship for her day, was outward bound on her third voyage to 'the Coast and Bombay', commanded by Captain Richard Pierce. She left the Thames on January 1st 1786, but encountered severe weather in the Channel and on the 4th a strong westerly gale caused her to ship a lot of water through the hawse-holes at her bows, the normal canvas cloths which covered these openings having been burst by the seas. In a short time she had seven feet of water in her hold and, weighed down, she was rolling dangerously. In fact the situation became so desperate that her captain decided he must lighten her by cutting away the mizen mast. Later the main mast was similarly cut away, but in so doing five seamen were carried overside by the tangle of tackle and drowned. When in sight of Berry Head they turned and bore up for Portsmouth. At noon on the 5th they saw Portland Bill to the north-east and driving too far to leeward to make Portland Roads, tried to get to Studland Bay.

Progress was painfully slow and uncertain under the improvised jury rig and they were largely at the mercy of the tides. Visibility was poor after nightfall, but an hour or so before midnight the weather cleared and they saw St. Alban's Head to leeward. They anchored, but dragged slowly shoreward, most of the time rolling heavily and yawing from side to side. Many went below to get a little shelter from the bitter cold and the waves which broke over them incessantly. They were driving ashore near a spot called Seacombe close to Winspit on the Peveril side of St. Alban's Head, but nobody was about in that desolate spot and they were unseen. At about two in the morning of the 6th they 'struck with such violence as to dash the heads of those who were standing in the cuddy against the deck above them . . . A shriek of horror burst at one instant from every quarter of the ship'. The scene must have been one of extreme despair, the bold cliff rising above them, the ship falling broadside on to the narrow rocky ledge beneath and quickly beating in her bilge. But just one glimmer of hope was afforded by a low wide-mouthed cavern at the foot of the cliffs. The *Halsewell* soon broke in-two pieces and Meriton, the Chief Officer, seized a chance to jump from the stern on to the rocks. He was probably the only one who reached shore in the darkness, but could find no way of climbing to the top or of helping his shipmates. Three hours later the dawn broke and others began to clamber and slither down to the rocks. As many as possible moved into the cavern, but its floor was flooded and there was disappointingly little room to cling to rock ledges at the sides and back. The cook and the quartermaster with great courage persevered painfully and slowly in climbing the cliff, and successful at last, made their way to the home of Garland, the steward to the proprietors of the quarries in the neighbourhood. He at once summoned a band of quarrymen, tough and accustomed to work on the cliffs, and they went to the scene with ropes and stakes.

The cavern was not visible from above, but of course they knew its location. At first they let their ropes down across its entrance out of reach of the unfortunates within. The noise of the gale drowned all shouts and it was some time before one or two men descended far enough to be able to indicate to those above the right spot. The ropes were dropped to the sides of the cave and the slow business began of hauling men to the top, one at a time. Many were so benumbed with shock and the cold they could not tie the rope around themselves or hold it tightly enough and so dropped into the icy water or on to the rocks below. Rescue work went on slowly but surely and it took 24 hours to bring up the last of the 74 survivors. It was estimated that another seventy had come ashore but died of cold or been washed away before they could be rescued. As the *Halsewell's* complement had been at least 240, a further hundred souls had been lost on the wreck itself. This was certainly another of the major catastrophes of the sea.

Above the tumbled boulders of St. Alban's Head are the galleries and the pathways cut by generations of stone masons. On top, close to the ruined chapel, is the row of Coastguard cottages and the shed for the rescue apparatus. There is also a modern look-out post which is constantly manned. Visualising the scene when the cottages were built, in 1827 they had a Manby mortar for life-saving purposes and in 1842 they were supplied with the far more convenient Dennett rockets. Late in 1838 and early in 1839 there were two outstanding rescues by the St. Alban's Head Coastguards in which they used their boats, presumably launched from Chapman's Pool. On the earlier occasion they saved the crew of seven of the *Aimable Mère*, bound from Bordeaux for Dunkirk. Lieutenant W. Parsons was awarded the Institution's silver medal and his seven boatmen rewarded. On the second occasion the same officer led six boatmen to save the crew of twelve of the brig *Fortitude*, bound from Bahia for Cowes.

Another famous stranding in this area, this time happily without loss of life, was that on January 13th 1857, when the iron paddle steamer *Tyne* struck between Chapman's Pool and Kimmeridge. Bound from Brazil for Southampton with 55 passengers, mails and a valuable cargo including diamonds valued at £32,548, cochineal and tapioca, and also two 'American lions', she encountered thick fog after sighting Portland lights at 2 in the morning. Although proceeding only at a quarter speed she grounded at about 3.30 on a bed of chalk and gravel and the impact was so heavy that people were thrown from their bunks. There were immediate scenes of near panic as the passengers rushed to the deck in their night-clothes. Little could be seen in the darkness and fog, but later it was realised they were about half a mile off a high cliff. The weather was quiet but there was a steady swell and the *Tyne* bumped for four hours before the tide rose and she became steadier.

Meanwhile passengers were assured there was no immediate danger

The salvage vessel Lyons *standing by the s.s.* Dorothea, *stranded on Chesil Beach in February 1914.* [*Photo: Eric Latcham Collection*]

The German liner Bulow *stranded in dense fog at Blacknor Point, Portland on June 18th 1914. She was later refloated.* [*Photo: Eric Latcham Collection*]

The Greek steamship Preveza drove ashore at Chesil Cove on January 15th 1920 and soon afterwards broke in two. She had to be broken up on the spot.
[Photo: Eric Latcham Collection]

The Royal Navy trawler James Fennell, *bound from Gibraltar for Portsmouth, drove ashore and became a total wreck near Chesil Cove on the day after the* Preveza— *January 16th 1920.* [*Photo: Eric Latcham Collection*]

The large French schooner Madeleine Tristan *was driven ashore at Chesil Cove in September 1930. Her hull remained high up on the beach here for several years.* [*Photo: Eric Latcham Collection*]

The barque County of
Anglesea developed a list
at sea in heavy weather
on February 26th 1905.
The Weymouth lifeboat
took off two men and
stood by whilst tugs
towed the barque to a
safe anchorage.
[Photo: Eric Latcham
Collection]

and persuaded to go below to dress while efforts were made to land the mails. Lieutenant Fuge, R.N., in charge of this important department, took a ship's boat to find a landing place, but they were capsized off a nearby beach. He met the local officer in charge of the Coastguard and obtained the use of the station boats to retrieve the mails, later accompanying them by coach to Southampton. H.M. steam frigate *Devastation* was sent from Portsmouth as well as tugs from Southampton and Portland, but by the time they arrived all the passengers had been landed by the ship's boats and taken to Corfe Castle where they were refreshed and rested at the home of Lord Eldon. It was found that the *Tyne*'s boilers had moved six inches forward on the impact of grounding and that the water was two feet deep in the saloon. It was impossible to move her that day so she was abandoned for the night. She was eventually refloated several weeks later, somewhat to everybody's surprise.

In the 1860's the lifeboat service was expanding rapidly and opportunities came to fill in the gaps between older stations. It was recommended that an 'Isle of Purbeck' station should be established and Chapman's Pool was chosen as being close to the broad headland on the one hand and Kimmeridge Ledges on the other. The Pool, a strange basin surrounded by dark cliffs was, and still is, a somewhat gloomy and remote spot. A few fishermen lived near the bay but a full crew necessitated enrolling men from a wide area. A boat house was built on the eastern side of the cove. An anonymous lady, known by the initials 'E.M.S.', sent £300 to Admiral Gambier for the lifeboat and this, the *George Scott*, was sent down from London by rail to Wareham in November 1866. She was a standard self-righting craft, 30 feet long, pulling ten oars, and was provided with a carriage even though the tracks of the neighbourhood were devious and steep and it would have entailed a long hard journey to any other launching place. As if to emphasise the remoteness of the Pool, the *George Scott* was first taken to Swanage for her christening by Lady Augusta Freemantle, sister of the Earl of Eldon.

What turned out to be the only service launch in the history of the station took place on September 25th 1868, when the schooner *Liberty*, of Portsmouth, was wrecked on Broad Bench on the western side of Kimmeridge Bay. Unfortunately the schooner slipped off the reef and sank in deep water, taking all hands with her, before either the Chapman's Pool lifeboat or the small Coastguard galley from Kimmeridge could reach the scene. This tragedy led the R.N.L.I. to establish a further lifeboat station at Kimmeridge, of which more later.

In spite of this setback the Chapman's Pool Station was retained. The shaly cliffs behind and on the landward side of the lifeboat house were unstable and on several occasions minor landslips caused damage to the various net- and boat-houses on the site. Because of this trouble the lifeboat house had to be partly rebuilt in 1876. Four years later, no further calls having been received, it was decided to discontinue the station. Since then further subsidence has swept away all traces of the former lifeboat house.

Kimmeridge, sometimes spelt with one 'M', consists of a wide bay at the foot of a valley leading to the attractive village of that name, a row of well-kept fishermen's cottages by the side of a stream leading to the shore being known as Goulter. The bay had been developed originally as a commercial harbour by Sir William Clavel in the late seventeenth century. His aim was to export the local shale for the extraction of train oil. However, the trade did not expand and to further dampen his enterprise Clavel's great stone quay, a hundred feet long, stretching halfway across the bay, was battered down by a great storm in 1745. In the middle nineteenth century another quay was built with a limekiln at its end, and most of this is still to be seen.

Along this part of the coast an extraordinary indraught has been noted. It is said that in December 1847, an American ship which had been struck by lightning many miles away off Ushant was driven ashore at Kimmeridge by wind and currents, a mass of flames. Her crew had escaped earlier in their boats. Again, when the mail steamship *Amazon* was burnt in the Bay of Biscay in January 1852, boats and wreckage were washed up hereabouts.

As already mentioned the lifeboat station was founded after the tragic wreck of the schooner *Liberty*. For many years there had been an active Coastguard station and the R.N.L.I. records show a rescue in 1838 when a Coastguard galley manned by Lieutenant Smith, R.N., and seven of his men, saved the eight-man crew of the French lugger *Joseph Desire*. Again in September 1856, five Coastguards saved the crew of four of the sloop *Carnarvon Castle* wrecked in hazy weather on Cuttle Ledge.

As there was a scarcity of competent men, apart from the Coast-guards, who were, of course, bound by regulations and not necessarily available, it was decided to send to Kimmeridge a small 28-feet lifeboat rowing five oars single banked. A donation of £200 from Benjamin Heape, of Manchester, was used to provide the boat and she was named *Mary Heape*. A sheltered spot was found where the boat could be launched even when it was impossible to get a boat off from any other part of the bay. At first she was kept under a canvas cover on a small level patch beneath the cliff, but a year later a wooden house was built at the head of a convenient gap in the low cliff.

The *Mary Heape*'s first service began at 11 p.m. on December 9th 1872, when the Norwegian full-rigged ship *Stralsund* was wrecked on the east side of the bay in a hurricane from the south-west. The lifeboat went out, but after a desperate struggle the five rowers were forced back on to the beach, being unable to stem the seas swirling round the eastern point of the bay. At daylight there was a slight improvement in the weather and they made a second attempt which proved successful. Using a line thrown over the wreck by the rocket apparatus, they hauled the lifeboat to and fro until the whole crew of fifteen were landed.

In the next few years there were at least four wrecks in the vicinity but the crews either got away in their own boats or were saved by the rocket apparatus. On August 18th 1877, the Caernarvon brigantine *Commodore*, with a cargo of slates for Hamburg, stranded on Enscombe Ledges in poor visibility and became a total loss. In similar circumstances on December 2nd 1878, the iron three-masted schooner *Gipsy Queen*, of Glasgow, bound from Navassa Island in the West Indies for Newcastle with guano, was wrecked on Kimmeridge Ledge. Again, a year later, on November 24th 1879, the Arbroath schooner *Catherine McIver*, bound from Par for Sunderland with china clay, was wrecked on the Ledges; and on November 19th 1880, the Glasgow steamer *Arklow*, bound for Southampton, was wrecked nearby.

It was felt that the Kimmeridge station needed a larger boat and by some means extra hands were found to man a 32-feet ten-oared craft which also took the name *Mary Heape*. Before her arrival in 1881 a larger wooden boat-house was built on the site of the old. There was, however, another wreck, this time at Warbarrow, on Christmas Day 1883, for which the lifeboat's services were not required. The Great Western Railway steamer *South of Ireland*—she had originally been employed between Milford and Waterford—was homeward bound from Cherbourg for Weymouth with a general cargo and a solitary passenger, when she stranded in foggy weather. Her crew of 23 and the passenger were saved, but the vessel could not be moved and became a total wreck.

The only service of the second *Mary Heape* came on March 21st 1886, when the little trading cutter *Ceres*, of Poole, with a cargo of barley from Truro, ran ashore in fog close to the lifeboat station. She had been hove to because of the fog when her crew realised she was drifting into danger and manoeuvred her head round to the south. Unfortunately the wind then changed and with this and the tide she was carried on to Broad Bench. Two men got into her boat to lay out an anchor with a view to kedging her off the rocks, but it capsized in the surf. One man was swept away and drowned after clinging to the boat's keel for some time, but the other managed to hold on to the oars until the lifeboat reached him. Afterwards the lifeboat went to the *Ceres* and with considerable difficulty, as the waves were sweeping right over her, saved the master and the other hand.

A couple of months later, on May 15th, the London steamer *Palala*, bound for Port Natal with general cargo and seven passengers, stranded on Kimmeridge Ledge. The 35 people on board got ashore safely, but the vessel could not be refloated and salvage work kept the local people busy for a long time.

In November 1887, the 34-feet self-righting lifeboat *Augustus Arkwright* was sent to the station, one of the latest pattern of water-ballasted lifeboats. Her inaugural ceremony was on May 9th 1888, when she was named after Captain Arkwright, sometime M.P. for North Derbyshire, by Mrs. Arkwright.

On January 11th 1890 the Padstow schooner *Minnie* stranded in the bay and became a total loss, her crew of four saving themselves in their own boat. Next the sole service of the new lifeboat took place on June 26th 1892, when the brigantine *Lythemore*, of Llanelly, ran on the Ledge in fog. She was bound from Cardiff for Southampton with coal, and was in a dangerous position bumping heavily in a ground sea, but miraculously she survived. After standing by all night the lifeboatmen laid out an anchor, and by this means the brigantine was kedged into deep water on the tide. She went on her way, her pumps being able to control the leakage.

A few years later it was decided that the Kimmeridge station was not needed and at a committee meeting at R.N.L.I. headquarters on February 13th 1896, it was decided to close forthwith. Subsequent casualties in this area were dealt with by the Weymouth and Swanage lifeboats.

There were, however, a number of later casualties in the immediate vicinity to which the lifeboats were not called or to which they were unable to give help. On the last day of 1898 the Rochester ketch *Ada*, bound in ballast from Southampton for Cherbourg stranded on Kimmeridge Beach in a severe southerly gale. On November 10th 1900, the London steamer *Hildegarde*, with Spanish iron ore for Newcastle, drove ashore at Freshwater and her heavy cargo contributed to her rapid disintegration. Also on November 14th 1909 the Jersey ketch *Morning Star*, with copper ore loaded at Calstock on the Tamar, stranded on Broad Bench and became a wreck. In none of these three cases were lives lost.

BOAT RECORD, CHAPMAN'S POOL AND KIMMERIDGE

Years on station	Length, Breadth, Oars/Crew	Type, Weight, Cost	Year built, (Off. no.), Builder	Boat's name, Donor, Authority
(a) at Chapman's Pool				
1866-1880	30' 7' 1" 10/13	SR 1t10 £248	1866 Forrestt, Limehouse	*George Scott,* E.M.S. (anonymous lady) R.N.L.I.
(b) at Kimmeridge				
1868-1881	28' 6' 8" 5/6	SR 1t5 £146	1868 Woolfe, Shadwell	*Mary Heape* Benj. Heape, Manchester R.N.L.I.
1881-1887	32' 7' 6" 10/12	SR 2t £287	1881 Woolfe, Shadwell	*Mary Heape* as above R.N.L.I.
1887-1896	34' 7' 6" 10/13	SR 3t10 £350	1887 (137) Forrestt, Limehouse	*Augustus Arkwright* F. C. Arkwright and family R.N.L.I.

SERVICE RECORD, CHAPMAN'S POOL AND KIMMERIDGE

(a) Chapman's Pool
Nil

(b) Kimmeridge
Mary Heape Lifeboat
1872 Dec. 9 Ship *Stralsund*, of Stralsund (Norway), saved   15

Mary Heape (second) Lifeboat
1886 Mar. 21 Cutter *Ceres*, of Poole, saved   3

Augustus Arkwright Lifeboat
1892 Jun. 26 Brigantine *Lythemore*, of Llanelly, stood by and assisted
to refloat

4

SWANAGE

THE SUMMER VISITOR out to enjoy the rugged beauty and superb views of Purbeck, might take the cliff path eastwards from St. Alban's Head. Passing Anvil Point and its lighthouse (dating from 1881), he would find that the tip of the *massif* ends in Durlston Head. Then there is a little bay ending in Peveril Point, the southern tip of the larger Swanage Bay. On the far side the cliffs again rise to nearly 400 feet in the vicinity of Ballard Point, the northern tip of the bay, remain high to the Foreland, alternatively known as Handfast Point, and then beyond to Studland Bay where the land drops abruptly almost to sea level. Off the Foreland lie the familiar rock pinnacles Old Harry and his Wife, the latter nearly demolished during a great storm in 1896.

The *Pilot's Handbook* is not enthusiastic about Swanage Bay as a sheltering place, for although it gives some shelter from westerlies any swing towards the east made conditions dangerous for sailing vessels. The dangers to shipping in general were stated to be the cliffs and the ledges at their feet, which in some parts stretch a considerable distance from the shore. The *Handbook* (dated 1866) also noted that Purbeck stone was shipped from the pier and one cannot help thinking that in the days before this stone traffic ended the little town must have presented a very different aspect from that of the popular resort we see now.

Early maritime activity in Swanage Bay included a hard fought sea fight in 877, when Alfred's navy defeated a Danish invasion fleet and a hundred or more galleys were driven on to the rocks at Peveril Point. However, coming down to more recent times we find that many of the casualties in the immediate vicinity of Swanage were vessels connected with the stone trade. In February 1791 the *Neptune*, Swanage for London, went 'on shore and bulged[1] near Pool'; in January 1793, the *Fanny*, for London, was 'lost off Purbeck, the crew saved'; in July 1802, the *Betsey*, bound for Arundel, was lost in Studland Bay, the captain

---

[1] Sometimes rendered as 'bilged'. It was a common expression in the days of wooden ships and meant that the hull had strained causing the lower planks to open up, so releasing the caulking and allowing the water to enter.

and two men drowned. There were, of course, other craft from farther afield, mainly of the coasting type, which stranded in the area, sometimes being lucky enough to be refloated later.

As to life-saving apparatus there was a Manby mortar at Swanage in 1827, and Dennett rockets were provided in 1842. The early reports of the Institution give several cases of rewards to Coastguards and others for rescue work hereabouts. The first was in November 1827, to two Coastguards and four seamen for the rescue of a sailor from the schooner *Sisters*, of Exeter, wrecked at Peveril Point. The other seven men on board the schooner were drowned and as this would make a very large crew for this class of vessel, one may assume they included some local men working as hovellers or trimmers. There was a famous rescue in April 1839, when the crew of eight of the French brig *Jean-Marie* was saved. On this occasion silver medals were awarded to Lieutenant George Davies, R.N., of the Coastguard, and to Gunner Edward Leggett and seaman Charles Stubbs of the revenue cruiser *Tartar*. Davies, later a Vice-Admiral, had a long and distinguished career in the Royal Navy and the Coastguard, later joining the R.N.L.I. as an Inspector, winning a gold and three silver medals for acts of gallantry on various occasions.

As we have seen, when considering lifeboat stations for the Isle of Purbeck the authorities thought that they should be placed on the south coast close to the great dangers of St. Alban's Head and Kimmeridge Ledges. However, on the night of January 23rd 1875, the brigantine *Wild Wave*, of Exeter, was thrown on to Peveril Ledge during a heavy gale. John Lose, the Chief Officer of the Coastguard, ordered out two four-oared gigs. One was to stand by, and the other, which he coxed, to endeavour to reach the wreck. In this they were frustrated by the tremendous breaking seas and the darkness. A rocket line was sent over from the shore, but as soon as it was fixed a particularly large sea threw the *Wild Wave* over on her beam ends and the line was carried under water, making it useless. Nothing more could be done until dawn when it was seen that five or six men—the accounts differ—were still alive on the wreck. In a further sustained effort the Coastguards got their boat alongside and rescued them. Moments later the brigantine slipped from the rock ledge and foundered in deep water. John Lose was awarded the R.N.L.I. silver medal and the twelve Coastguards who took part in various rescue attempts were also rewarded.

Following this wreck a petition was sent to the R.N.L.I. asking them to establish a lifeboat at Swanage, and at a committee meeting on March

4th 1875, this was agreed. There was available a sum of money passed to the Institution by Samuel J. Wilde, of Serjeant's Inn, being an amount his late aunt, Miss Margaret Ryder Wilde, had asked him to give the R.N.L.I. for a lifeboat to be named *Charlotte Mary* in memory of her late sisters. The Earl of Eldon gave a plot of land at a convenient site and here a lifeboat house was built for £350, together with a slipway for an additional £175. There was a public inauguration on September 16th, when the lifeboat was named by Mrs. Wilde.

The first service of the station came just over a year later on September 30th 1876, when a sudden heavy south-easterly gale caught two vessels at anchor in a dangerous position in the bay. The lifeboat took five from the London schooner *Maid of Kent*, and two from the local yacht *Dragon*. Later in the day the wind veered to the south and moderated, enabling the lifeboat to put back the schooner's crew who, with some lifeboatmen assisting, were able to take her into Poole. On November 11th following, the smack *Aries* was dragging her anchors in a gale from the E.S.E. Again the lifeboat put four men on board who slipped her cables, made sail, and took her to a sandy part of the bay where she could take the ground without risk.

On January 7th 1879, a messenger from Studland said there was a vessel in distress near the entrance to Poole harbour, and although this was some distance to the east, the prevailing wind made it easier for the Swanage boat to reach the casualty than the Poole boat. They found that the Portsmouth ketch *Effort* had parted her anchor cables and been driven ashore near South Haven Point where she lay with the seas making a clean breach over her. With great difficulty they got alongside, took off the crew of two and then landed them at Poole.

Not long after this rescue there were two strandings at Ballard Point in quick succession. Early on January 17th the historic American naval frigate *Constitution*, at that time a sea-going training ship with a nominal rating of six guns, became lost in dense fog and grounded on a rocky ledge. The weather was quiet and a boat was sent ashore with a message which resulted in the naval tug *Malta* being sent to the spot. The frigate floated off the rocks at 3.30 on the same afternoon and, sturdy wooden wall that she was, a subsequent dry-docking at Portsmouth showed she had lost only a part of her false keel and loosened her rudder fastenings.

A week later, at 2 in the morning of the 24th the Norwegian barque *Anne Margrethe*, bound from Rouen for Baltimore, also stranded at Ballard Point. She was not so lucky. There was a north-easterly breeze

A dramatic photograph of the Weymouth lifeboat Friern Watch *approaching the schooner* Ardente, *from which she saved the crew of four on December 11th 1914.*   [*Photo: Eric Latcham Collection*]

The Malouin fishing ketch L'Arguenon *dragged her anchors until she stranded on Weymouth Sands on Christmas Day, 1930.* [*Photo: Eric Latcham Collection*]

The 51-foot Barnett-class motor lifeboat William and Clara Ryland *had a magnificent record at Weymouth from 1930 to 1957, saving 135 lives.*

with a heavy swell and, being in ballast, she soon pounded to pieces. The master, his daughter, and crew of ten were brought ashore, six in the ship's boat and six in a Coastguard boat.

On April 29th 1882, there was a tragedy to the west of Swanage when the full-rigged ship *Alexandrovna*, owned at Liverpool, although registered at St. John, New Brunswick, was driven ashore near Tilly Whim between Winspit and Anvil Point lighthouse during a hurricane from the S.S.W. She was bound in ballast from Maasluis in Holland for Cardiff, and was first seen approaching the coast at four in the afternoon. The lifeboat crew were mustered, but it was realised that there was no hope whatever of rounding Durlston Head in the prevailing conditions. Accordingly they remained standing by to launch if by chance a ship's boat or wreckage with survivors was swept into Durlston Bay. Meanwhile the rocket apparatus was manhandled along the cliff path to the scene, but there was no response to shouts or signals, and it seemed the wreck had been abandoned. The lifeboat crew stood down when it became dark and re-mustered promptly at dawn. They then launched in marginally better weather conditions to investigate the mystery. They could see no sign of life on the wreck although they were unable to approach very closely owing to the rocks. After carefully observing the cliffs and rocks on each side for any sign of life, they returned. The ship is believed to have had a crew of eighteen, all of whom were lost, and to have struck and broken into pieces in ten minutes. Her name was unknown until an empty ship's boat was found off Yarmouth in the Isle of Wight, and large quantities of wreckage were thrown ashore by the tide near the Needles.

The last two services of the *Charlotte Mary* were in 1883, when they remained all night by the yacht *Thalia* moored in a very dangerous position, and saved her crew of five at dawn; and in 1889, when they took the crew of four from the schooner *William Maskill*, stranded at Old Harry Ledge. This crew was landed at Studland so that they could watch for an opportunity to reboard the vessel, but she became a total loss. She had been on passage from Jersey for Southampton with the somewhat unusual cargo of coal tar and grease. There were three other casualties in the area in this period, in one of which, on Boxing Day 1886, the Newport brigantine *Forest Queen* stranded near Anvil Point and her crew of six were drowned in attempting to reach shore in their boat. She was bound from Antwerp for Silloth with phosphate and came ashore in a severe (force 9) gale from the south-east. The other wrecks were not attended by loss of life. The Spanish steamer *Mayo* was on passage from Rotterdam for Bilbao in a light condition and was blown ashore in a hurricane on November 1st 1887, at the western side of St. Alban's Head.

In December 1890, a new and larger lifeboat, 37-feet and twelve-oared, was sent to Swanage. She was the *William Erle*, presented by Lady Erle in memory of her late husband Chief Justice Sir William Erle. The boat was of the latest pattern with two drop-keels and three water-ballast tanks which were automatically filled on entering the sea. Unfortunately the Swanage men did not take to the new boat, saying she lacked stability, and three years later she was replaced without having had a single service launch.

The first service call of the new *William Erle*, on January 12th 1895, turned into tragedy. She was launched in the early afternoon to the Norwegian barque *Brilliant* which was in distress near the Hook Sand off Poole Harbour. The wind, of gale force, was S.E. by E., a dangerous quarter, and there were frequent flurries of snow. The lifeboat made good progress, however, until they were off Old Harry, where the strong ebb tide running out against the wind over the ledges made a terribly confused race. A series of high waves came up on her quarter and she broached-to. Although she recovered quickly without actually capsizing, men and gear had been washed from end to end and two were missing overboard. Thomas Marsh was seen close by and quickly hauled back, but Coxswain William Brown was a considerable distance away. The confusion on board was tremendous and in spite of all their efforts, by the time they had the oars and other gear put back in place, the coxswain had disappeared from sight. Attempts to get under sail were frustrated by damage to the foremast and by then they had drifted dangerously close to the cliffs. The second coxswain, faced with an agonising decision, had to turn about and make for Swanage. The Poole lifeboat was able to save the crew of the *Brilliant*, as will be told later.

The *William Erle's* first rescue came on April 6th 1897, when she saved two Coastguards in a water-logged punt which was being swept to sea. The men had put off to investigate wreckage off Peveril Point, but were caught by the race and capsized. Skilled boatmen as they were, they righted the boat, but she was so low in the water that it was a hopeless task to bale her out. The lifeboat reached them after a long hard pull at the oars.

The *William Erle* was away from station during November 23-24th 1898, and for part of this time was manned by Poole lifeboatmen. The complex series of services began with a phone message from Studland that a three-masted schooner was in a dangerous position off the village and signalling for help. A whole southerly gale was blowing with heavy seas breaking on the beaches and over the shallows. The lifeboat found she was the *Velocity*, of Leith, bound from Shields for Poole with coal, riding heavily at her anchors and badly strained so that she was leaking. Her master did not wish to abandon the vessel and in the prevailing conditions the coxswain could not put men on board to help at the pumps. As the water was shallow, at low tide the schooner would inevitably begin to bump and probably break up. So the coxswain decided to anchor the lifeboat in smoother water nearby and keep watch. The Poole lifeboat came out but returned when she saw the Swanage crew at the scene. At about ten in the evening the schooner showed signals of distress again and it was found that, having parted one anchor cable, she was drifting farther inshore. With great difficulty the crew of six were taken off. Entering Poole Harbour, they took on board a Poole lifeboatmen as a pilot, arriving at Poole Quay at three in the morning. The schooner became a total wreck on the patch known as Ball's Sand.

A few hours later the Poole lifeboat went out to the Norwegian three-masted schooner *Frier*, in distress to the east of the harbour entrance, and soon afterwards word came that yet another vessel was signalling for provisions off Christchurch Ledge. The Swanage crew, having been at sea for nearly twelve hours, were too exhausted to go out again, so the Poole reserve crew took out the *William Erle* and found the French barque *Bonne Mère*. The provisions were put on board the barque and her master, knowing he was anchored in a very dangerous position, asked them to obtain the services of a tug and twelve men. This was done, the Poole lifeboat also coming to assist. The Frenchmen not wishing to leave their vessel both lifeboats returned to Poole at about nine in the evening. The next day the Swanage lifeboat was brought back to her station.

The following three services of the *William Erle* were to pleasure craft; the *Bluebell*, which broke from her moorings, and the *Florinda*, which was riding dangerously close to the cliffs at Wanspit with one man aboard. The steam yacht *Ilona* was ashore at St. Alban's Head in thick fog, but was saved by tugs with the lifeboat's help. They were called out in the very early hours of January 27th 1909, and found that five of the yacht's crew had taken to their boat, leaving the captain on board. However, after rowing a few hours they became lost in the fog and had some grimly anxious moments before they got back to the yacht. Then they found they could not get aboard again as the yacht was rolling heavily and unpredictably, pivoting while held on the rocks by her forefoot. They were in this position for three hours and were so cold, frightened and exhausted, that the lifeboat first landed them at Chapman's Pool, returning to stand by the yacht until the tugs arrived.

The next service came on April 22nd 1914, when the London steam coaster *Envermeu* went ashore on the rocks west of St. Alban's Head in thick fog. So dense was the fog, in fact, that the lifeboat searched for six hours, not finding her until two in the morning of the 23rd. The Kimmeridge Coastguard had also asked for two tugs from Weymouth and these arrived at about the same time. They stood by until high water but it was then found there was too much water in the *Envermeu's* hold, and the refloating attempt failed. The steamer was lying easily and not in immediate danger so the lifeboat returned.

In the following month the *William Erle* was condemned and sold, her place being taken temporarily by the reserve lifeboat *Zaida*, a 37-feet ten-oared self-righting boat built in 1896 for Carrickfergus in Ireland.

The only wartime service of the station was performed by the *Zaida* on the evening of April 25th 1915, when she went to a vessel showing signals of distress in Swanage Bay. She proved to be the London barge *Maggie*, bound from Alderney for Newport, Isle of Wight, with granite. Her two-man crew were exhausted with pumping and about to leave her, but with five lifeboatmen to help, the water was considerably reduced in an hour. With the flood tide they then took the barge into Poole Harbour, eventually putting her ashore in a safe place, the water having by then once more risen to the cabin floor.

The station was closed for a short while in 1917, so many local men being in the services, but was reopened in August 1918, with the new 37½-feet self-righting *Herbert Sturmy*. The boat had been on order since 1914 but her completion had been delayed by the war and, as it turned out, she was one of the last three sailing and pulling lifeboats taken into the R.N.L.I. fleet.

The *Herbert Sturmy's* first service, on May 23rd 1920, proved to be the only occasion on which she actually saved life while on this station. She went out to a small pleasure boat which was drifting to sea on a strong ebb tide much to the consternation of her occupants, a lady and gentleman. On the way out the lifeboat found a small motor boat, also with two people, broken down. Both boats and four thankful amateur sailors were brought back to land.

The remaining services of the *Herbert Sturmy* during her ten years on the station included standing by the steam drifter *Free Will*, ashore on Peveril Ledges in dense fog; and the barges *Cetus* and *Carson* in a dangerous position off the entrance to Poole Harbour. On April 9th 1927, she stood by the French cargo ketch *Kelloch*, aground at Peveril Point while on passage from Leith for Poole, with coal.

To accommodate a motor lifeboat alterations costing over £6,000 were made to the house and slipway. The *Thomas Markby* was a 40-feet self-righting lifeboat with a 40-horse power engine formally named on July 7th 1928 before a crowd of six thousand spectators. Her first service, on January 5th following, was to the coasting steamship *Grosvenor*, which went ashore at Kimmeridge while bound from Swansea for Portsmouth, with a cargo of flour. Called out in mid-afternoon, the lifeboat found the steamer rolling in a heavy swell. She took a hawser to a waiting tug, but it was not a suitable time of tide to refloat. They stood by through a bitterly cold night and on the morning tide the steamer floated free, but with a heavy list to port. Her crew called urgently for the lifeboat and as she drew alongside six jumped in at once. However, the *Grosvenor's* engineers pumped water out of various portside tanks and she almost righted herself. Thus reassured some of the crew returned, and she steamed slowly to Portland with the tug and lifeboat escorting. The lifeboatmen were on service twenty hours.

Later in the same year the *Thomas Markby* saved the two occupants of the yacht *Gwynedd* in distress in Studland Bay. In 1932 she saved the Poole fishing boat *Redwing*, dismasted and with her engine broken down, after a night search which ended a long way to the east, off Boscombe Pier. Many of the subsequent services were to pleasure craft and in July 1933 there were two within a month. In the case of the *Skylark*, the motor launch was found to have been taken in tow by the well-known paddle steamer *Lorna Doone*, off Bournemouth Pier, and was passed to the lifeboat for towing to Poole.

In 1934, a year in which the Swanage lifeboat accomplished six services, an unusual total which was not to be surpassed until 1960, there was an outstanding case when a yachtsman was saved by an act of individual bravery. Soon after noon on March 19th the Southbourne Coastguard reported a small yacht in difficulties in a strong southerly gale and heavy sea. In an hour after launching the lifeboat came up to the yacht *Hally Lise* with a doctor from Chicago and a Frenchman on board. Their jib sail had been blown away and they were unable to beat against the wind to get out to sea. A couple of hundred yards away was

Boscombe beach upon which eight-feet waves were breaking. As the lifeboat approached the yacht capsized and the Frenchman was washed overboard. He seized a piece of wreckage, but it was torn from his grasp, and he went under. The Assistant Motor Mechanic, Robert Brown, without hesitation jumped into the sea in his boots, oilskins and lifejacket. At that moment he could not see the submerged man but as he shook off his sea boots he made contact with him under water. He then brought him to the surface and both were picked up. The rescued man was unconscious for twenty minutes but recovered completely after a day in hospital. The American owner of the yacht was dragged ashore holding a rocket line sent over by the Coastguard. Robert Brown was awarded the bronze medal of the R.N.L.I.

As we have noted, many of the services until the outbreak of war were to pleasure craft. An exception was that on April 21st 1935, when they saved the trawler *Norman Craig*. She was on passage from Shoreham for Fleetwood, but had sought refuge in Swanage Bay to repair her rigging. Two of her crew of five were brought ashore by the second coxswain, who happened to be out in his boat, and he reported that the trawler was in a bad way. She had in fact lost her main anchor, and the small kedge they were using was not holding. She was also leaking and could not be pumped out as the auxiliary motor had broken down. The only thing to do was to tow the *Norman Craig* to Poole where she could be put on the grid-iron for repairs. There was another case, on August 5th 1936, when the lifeboat towed in the small steam coaster *Record*, bound from Portsmouth for Weymouth, which had been drifting off St. Alban's Head with her engine broken down.

A service of nearly twelve hours on July 4th 1937, for most of the time fighting a seventy-miles-an-hour gale, took the *Thomas Markby* much farther west than usual. It happened that the Weymouth lifeboat was undergoing repairs and could not attend to this call. At about 4.30 in the morning distress rockets had been reported five miles west of Portland Bill at a time when a moderate south-westerly gale was blowing, creating a very heavy sea. The Admiralty sent their tug *St. Just* from Portland base and the Swanage lifeboat was launched. The tug, much nearer to begin with, reached the scene first and found the yacht *Pauamma*, a yawl-rigged converted ship's lifeboat, bound for Yarmouth, disabled by the loss of her jib and mainsail. The tug held the yacht head to sea until the lifeboat arrived to take over the tow. In the very confused seas of the race the towrope parted twice but eventually the *Pauamma* and her two occupants were brought to a safe anchorage at

Weymouth. The lifeboat got back to Swanage at 4.20 in the afternoon.

The first service at Swanage after the outbreak of war was not to an actual war casualty, but as at most places on the south and east coasts it was accomplished while all boat movements were complicated by naval control. Soon after eight in the morning the Swanage Coastguard reported the Greek steamer *Turkie* ashore in the vicinity of Hounstout Cliff to the west of Chapman's Pool, but said she had made no signal for help. The Naval Headquarters at Portland sent out a tug and a drifter to take off the crew, but although there was a heavy swell causing their ship to grind ominously on the rocks, the Greeks thought there was a chance of saving her and would not leave. At seven in the evening the naval authorities gave permission for the lifeboat to launch and they found the *Turkie* then bumping heavily. The naval salvage officer asked them to stand by while efforts were made to tow the steamer off, and they remained nearby until four in the afternoon of the next day. It was then necessary for the lifeboat to return to refuel and for the crew to have a meal. She went out again two hours later and stood by until eleven the next morning. In all she was on duty 74 hours over four days, standing-by, transferring salvage parties from tugs to casualty, and *vice versa* fetching Lloyd's Agent from Kimmeridge, and finally, when all had failed, taking off the crew of 26 with their kits.

At a quarter past six on the evening of July 21st 1940, the Coastguard reported a vessel on fire some ten miles off in a southerly direction. Happily, the official procedure had by then been streamlined and the lifeboat was launched in less than a quarter of an hour. Forging south at full speed in a fairly calm sea, she found the Norwegian motor tanker *Kollskegg* ablaze forward after attack by enemy aircraft. The Norwegians had already been rescued by a destroyer, but the lifeboat stood by until a tug arrived to take the tanker in tow, some lifeboatmen being put on board to help make fast the wires.

Just after this came the 'Battle of Britain' and the Channel became the scene of aerial conflicts ranging from individual 'dogfights' to full scale battles. One such great battle was being fought at about five in the afternoon of August 25th 1940, in the Weymouth and Swanage areas. As we have already noted the Weymouth lifeboat could find no survivors or significant wreckage, but the *Thomas Markby*, going out to a report of four aircraft shot down about five miles off, found wreckage and clothing which was brought back for identification purposes.

Besides the successful services in 1940 there were no less than ten other launches which turned out to be fruitless and often long-drawn searches. Five of these were in that crowded August of 1940, and nine were on account of aircraft, including a drifting barrage balloon.

The outstanding service of the war for the Swanage station was that to the Free French Navy motor gunboat *Chasseur 5* on December 21st 1943. This small unit was escorting a British submarine in heavy seas when she capsized about three miles south of Durlston Head. The submarine radioed the N.O.I.C. (Naval Officer in Charge) at Poole who asked for the Swanage lifeboat at about 10.30 in the morning. Going out in an increasing south-westerly wind with poor visibility, the lifeboat came to the scene in three-quarters of an hour. Three sailors were clinging to the keel, two in a very shocked and exhausted state and they were quickly rescued when the coxswain skilfully manoeuvred the lifeboat close to the heaving hull. Four others had been rescued by the submarine with lines, but sixteen were trapped within the vessel, some of whom could be seen looking out of the portholes. With no tools to break into the hull, even supposing someone could be boarded on the slippery whale-like mass, they were helpless. A proposal for the submarine to ram the gunboat in an attempt to right her was abandoned as being too dangerous. The coxswain then asked the submarine commander to stand by while the lifeboat returned to Swanage. Returning with axes and saws they were unfortunately too late, for the vessel had sunk about half an hour earlier, and the submarine was already on her way to Portland.

The Coxswain and his crew of five received letters of thanks from the Commander-in-Chief of the Free French Naval Forces, and after the war all received medals from the French Government. The French lifeboat society (Société Centrale de Sauvetage des Naufragés) awarded Coxswain Robert Brown its silver gilt medal, and its bronze medal to Mechanic Alfred Chinchen and Bowman W. E. Nineham.

The remaining wartime service of the *Thomas Markby* was a search in the early hours of January 26th 1944, for survivors of an aircraft which had crashed three miles west of Hengistbury Head, but they found only some clothing and wreckage.

The first rescue after the war also had a connection with the conflict for it concerned one of the ubiquitious American 'Liberty' ships which were aiding the magnificent work done towards rehabilitating Europe. The *T. A. Johnston* went aground at Egmont Point, just west of Chapman's Pool, in foggy weather on the evening of December 10th 1945. Little could be done at the time but the master asked the lifeboat to stand by through the night and this was done. In the morning two tugs and a salvage vessel arrived, but their efforts were unavailing, and in fact one of the tugs also grounded. By then the tide was falling so operations had to be suspended, and the lifeboat returned for fuel and food for the crew. She went out again in the evening of the 11th to stand by all night and into the next day. The tug refloated herself, but the steamship remained fast. Later a signal was arranged for the lifeboat to come out immediately if her services were required again.

After a few more services to small pleasure craft the *Thomas Markby* came to the end of a useful career of 21 years, during which she had been launched 67 times, saved 27 lives, and helped countless other persons to safety. She was in fact still in excellent condition and spent a further nine years or so in the reserve fleet. The new Swanage lifeboat was of the 41-feet Watson Cabin class, a fine up-to-date craft with two 35 h.p. petrol engines and twin screws. She is still on the station and was, in 1962, fitted with new diesel engines to increase her speed and radius of action. She has a capacity for about 65 persons in rough weather and many more in fine weather. Her name—*R.L.P.*—was chosen by her donor, the late Mrs. Alice Pugh, of Kensington.

The first service launch of the *R.L.P.* came on the night of September 4th 1949, but after being given by radio several different positions for the casualty, she found the Weymouth lifeboat had already taken the disabled yacht *Lilida* in tow. However, her chance came on the afternoon of April 16th following, when a Coastguard message said a Vampire aircraft had crashed into the sea and the pilot had parachuted down about eight miles off Durlston Head. Fortunately, it was calm and the lifeboat was in time to save him, later transferring him to a naval launch.

Several services to small craft followed, details of which are in the service record. They included a brief spell of standing by a large schooner-rigged yacht, the *Lamorna*, which was bound for the Caicos Islands to seek Captain Kidd's reputed treasure. At the time the yacht was in tow of H.M. frigate *Redpole*, and in no immediate danger, but after the lifeboat had been dismissed, the yacht broke adrift. The Yarmouth lifeboat was by then the nearest to the casualty and went out to save the crew of fourteen before the yacht drove ashore, dismasted, near Christchurch. Another noteworthy service by the *R.L.P.* was on the afternoon of October 1st 1952, when they went out to the steam salvage vessel *Abide* which had been collecting scrap from the remains of the *Treveal*, wrecked, as recounted in the Weymouth chapter, as long ago as January 1920. The *Abide* was found aground on Freshwater

Ledge and rolling heavily in the swell. After towing for a while the life-boat freed her from the reef and took her to Swanage Bay where she was beached to caulk various leaking seams in the hull.

An outstanding service took place on the afternoon of December 12th 1955 when the Liverpool tug *Flying Kestrel* sent out a distress call as she had lost her tow—the barge *Sandheap*, off Poole Bar Buoy. The barge was drifting shorewards in a very rough sea with a gale from the E.S.E., with one man on board. Coxswain Robert Brown took the *R.L.P.* round Old Harry Rocks to Studland Bay and saw the barge aground on the Milkmaid Shoal, with seas breaking right over her. He took a wide sweep and approached with wind and sea astern, steadied on his course by the drogue streaming aft. He had to approach the weather side as there was not enough depth of water under her lee. Even then he found he was striking the bottom and the breaking seas tended to throw the lifeboat against the barge. It was then thought better to anchor and veer down to the barge stern-first, manoeuvring into position by skilful use of the engines so that the lone seaman could jump down to safety. This done, he was landed at Poole. The lifeboat herself had to remain there three days as the weather was too bad for rehousing at Swanage—a situation which often prevails in winter months. Coxswain Brown was awarded the formal Thanks inscribed on Vellum for the good seamanship and sound judgement he had shown in this rescue.

On July 29th 1956, the lifeboat made one of her shortest sorties for life-saving purposes—just half a mile off the launching slip. There was a very rough sea caused by a fresh westerly gale blowing against the tide and the four occupants of the small yacht *Onega* were in considerable danger as their anchor was dragging. It would have been dangerous to tie up alongside so the lifeboat made two passes, each time collecting two people, then bringing them back to the pier. She had to remain afloat until the weather moderated later in the day.

Other yacht services followed, the *Melanie* from Chapman's Pool; *Miss Britanny* off St. Alban's Head; the *Janice* six and a half miles out; *Solent Shirl* two miles off Anvil Point; the *William III* off Poole Harbour—in all cases the boat and her crew being towed to safety. Early on September 30th 1958, the lifeboat was launched a few hours after midnight to the yacht *Farida* which had run short of petrol on passage from Cherbourg for Hamble. The Dutch tanker *Capricornus* had re-layed the distress call and was standing by the yacht some seven and a half miles off Durlston Head in a gale and very rough sea. The lifeboat took her in tow and returned to Swanage at 4.15 in the morning. The weather then began to worsen and the wind backed to the south-east, causing the moored yacht's anchor to drag. She again showed distress signals and the lifeboat was launched soon after nine. By then the *Farida* was dangerously close to the shore, and as her fairleads had been damaged it would be impossible to moor her securely. Accordingly she was towed to Poole where she could be taken to the quay and repaired. The lifeboat had to stay at Poole for two days until the weather moderated enough to rehouse her at Swanage.

Soon after ten in the evening of March 29th 1960, the *R.L.P.* was launched following a report that a motor coaster was ashore west of St. Alban's Head, but in no immediate danger. There was a light wind and smooth sea, but it was very dark, and on nearing the vicinity the lifeboat sent up two parachute flares in succession to help her locate the casualty, which was found to be in Chapman's Pool. The *Magrix*, which had been on passage from Plymouth for her home port of Hull, was well ashore with her bows in the air, but her master radioed confidently 'We are sitting comfortably'. The frigate *Chichester* and a motor minesweeper came from Portland, and a large Dutch salvage tug from Southampton. The life-saving apparatus team established themselves nearby on the cliffs and all stood by to wait the rising tide in the morning. When this came it needed only a little towing by the tug to free the *Magrix* and her master's optimism was borne out when it was found there was only a slight leak in the forepeak. She had lain on a flat ledge but narrowly missed two large rocks which were on either side of her bows.

On March 10th 1962, there was a casualty which turned into a long-drawn salvage operation. Soon after three in the morning the Coastguard on top of St. Alban's Head realised that a vessel had gone ashore almost exactly below his lookout. He could not see her as there was fog and drizzling rain, but he at once informed the lifeboat secretary. The lifeboat was launched into a moderate sea and found the motor sand dredger *Sand Dart* on the rocks, bumping heavily with the swell. She had been on a ballast passage from Plymouth for Portsmouth. Five of the crew were taken off at the master's request but he stayed aboard with the mate and engineer to do what was possible towards salvage. The immediate fear was that she might not be on a flat bed and would roll over as the tide fell. The Coastguards came down the cliff with ropes and ladders and passed a line aboard by which the three men could escape if necessary. The coastal tanker *Esso Lyndhurst* approached to offer a tow, but the *Sand Dart* was already settling down, more or less level, but wedged between rocks amidships. The lifeboat went out a second time at about 10.30 in the morning and helped in connecting towing wires between the tanker and the casualty, but the ebbing tide frustrated all attempts to tow her off. During the following day the *Sand Dart* pounded heavily at high tide and visiting salvage experts found her hold had filled with the waves breaking over her rails, and her engine room had filled through leaks in her bottom. Salvage prospects looked grim, but some rocks were blasted away, motors were put on board to pump and the accessible leaks were stopped. Fortunately calm weather prevailed, the swell decreased and the vessel remained steady. However, there was no success on the next high tides in April and then gales blew up which drove her farther ashore. Early in the morning of May 25th, when there was nobody on the wreck, fire broke out. By a happy mischance a signal rocket was ignited and this warned the Coastguard. Firemen were brought quickly to the scene as the salvors had left gelignite on board to blast rocks, but fortunately this was saved before the fire got near. They extinguished the fire in a few hours after the bridge and accommodation were completely gutted. the heat having twisted steel beams and partitions out of shape. It now looked a hopeless case for salvage but the little ship was strongly built, and the salvors were not the sort to give up easily. They finally refloated her on October 14th, and towed her to Portland to be beached and patched. Some months later she was taken back to her builders' yard at Appledore for complete repairs.

During the winter of 1962-3 the *R.L.P.* was fitted with direction-finding equipment and an opportunity came to test it in operational conditions on the morning of June 4th 1963. The Coastguard reported that the French yacht *Stellar* had suffered an engine breakdown some twenty miles off Poole. The lifeboat was launched at nine and went off in calm weather finding the yacht had drifted to a position fourteen miles S.S.E. of Anvil Point, rather farther out in the Channel than the Swanage men usually went on rescue missions. Shortly before she reached the yacht, however, the Poole motor fishing vessel *Purbeck Isle* came up and took the disabled yacht in tow. The *Stellar* had three persons on board and was on a passage from Cherbourg. The Admiralty tug *Beagle* came out from Portland to assist, but was recalled when told that the rescue was in hand.

Among a number of rescues of cliff climbers which appear in the records in recent years the Swanage crew played a major part in saving a man who had been trapped for two days in a cave at Warbarrow Head. The rescuers ashore and afloat were seriously hampered by fog, and when Mr. G. A. Plant of the Lulworth Life-saving Company and Police Constable Pearce, of Wool, eventually reached the man it was found necessary to lower him to the water's edge where he was picked up in a rubber dinghy controlled by lines from the lifeboat. The official Thanks of the Institution was awarded collectively to Coxswain Brown and his crew.

Another class of service which is common on some parts of the coast, but rare at stations in Dorset, is the landing of sick or injured persons from passing vessels. One such case at Swanage on December 1st 1966, involved the Syrian motor vessel *Maya*. In the early afternoon the vessel came to anchor in Swanage Bay and hoisted a signal calling for a doctor. There was a southerly gale, rough sea and frequent rain squalls. The lifeboat reached the *Maya* in seven minutes from launching and found she was dragging her anchors while she rolled heavily in the swell. On the coxswain's suggestion the *Maya* raised her anchor and moved to another part of the bay where, the wind having veered through west to north-west, she would get a little shelter. The doctor and a lifeboatman, a qualified first-aider, were put on board with great difficulty owing to the liveliness of both craft. The doctor diagnosed an internal complaint and the sick man was strapped into a Neil Robertson stretcher for lowering into the lifeboat, while the wireless operator radioed for an ambulance to be waiting ashore. Dr. Aitken was awarded a special letter of Thanks on vellum in recognition of his help in difficult circumstances on this occasion.

The later services at Swanage to the time of writing have been to small craft, to swimmers, skin-divers and cliff climbers, all of which are part of the modern life-saving scene.

BOAT RECORD, SWANAGE

Years on station	Length, Breadth, Oars/Crew	Type, Weight, Cost	Year built, (Off. no.), Builder	Boat's name, Donor, Authority
1875-1890	35' 9' 10/13	SR 3t £389	1875 (193) Forrestt, Limehouse	*Charlotte Mary* Late Miss M. R. Wilde, R.N.L.I.　　　　[London
1890-1893	37' 8' 12/15	SR 4t10 £533	1890 (296) Watkins, Blackwell	*William Erle* Lady Erle of Liphook R.N.L.I.
1893-1914	37' 9' 12/15	SR 4t13 £584	1893 (358) Woolfe, Shadwell	*William Erle* as above R.N.L.I.
1914-1918	37' 9' 3" 10/13	SR 4t8 £492	1896 (392)[1] Hansen, Cowes	*Zaida* (reserve) Anonymous R.N.L.I.
1918-1928	37' 6" 9' 3" 12/15	SR 5t £2000	1918 (664) Saunders[2], E. Cowes	*Herbert Sturmy* Legacy Mrs. Sturmy, R.N.L.I.　　　[Blackheath
1928-1949	40' 10' 6" 10/9	SR(M) 11t14 £6559	1928 (706) Saunders, E. Cowes	*Thomas Markby* Legacy Mrs. G. H. Markby, R.N.L.I.　　　[Willesden
1949-	41' 11' 3" -/7	W(M) 14t12 £15584	1949 (858) Sussex Yacht Co., Shoreham	*R.L.P.* Legacy Mrs. Alice Pugh, R.N.L.I.　　　[Kensington

Notes　[1] Originally stationed at Carrickfergus, Ireland.
　　　　[2] Begun by Summers and Payne, completed by S. E. Saunders.

SERVICE RECORD, SWANAGE

Charlotte Mary Lifeboat
1876	Sep.	30	Schooner *Maid of Kent*, of London, saved	5
			Yacht *Dragon*, of Swanage, saved	2
			Schooner *Maid of Kent*, (second launch), saved vessel	
	Nov.	11	Smack *Aries*, of Cowes, saved vessel	
1879	Jan.	7	Ketch *Effort*, of Portsmouth, saved	2
1883	Sep.	1	Yacht *Thalia*, of Portsmouth, saved	5
1889	Mar.	7	Schooner *William Maskill*, of Goole, saved	4

William Erle Lifeboat
1897	Apr.	6	A Coastguard punt, saved	2
1898	Nov.	23	Schooner *Velocity*, of Leith, saved	6

(See Poole Service Record for services carried out by this lifeboat with a Poole crew on November 24th 1898).

1903	Sep.	9	Pleasure boat *Bluebell*, of Swanage, saved boat	
1905	Nov.	13	Yacht *Florinda*, of Portsmouth, saved yacht and	1
1909	Jan.	27	Steam yacht *Ilona*, of Glasgow, saved	5
1914	Apr.	22	Steamship *Envermeu*, of London, stood by	

Reserve Lifeboat
1915	Apr.	25	Barge *Maggie*, of London, assisted to save barge and	5

Herbert Sturmy Lifeboat

1920	May	23	A pleasure boat, of Swanage, saved boat and	2
			A small motor yacht, saved yacht and	2
1921	Oct.	8	Steam drifter *Free Will*, of Weymouth, stood by	
1923	Oct.	27	Barge *Cetus*, of London, stood by	
			Barge *Carson*, of Yarmouth, stood by	
1927	Apr.	9	Ketch *Kelloch* (French), stood by	

Thomas Markby Lifeboat

1929	Jan.	5-6	Steamship *Grosvenor*, of Lancaster, assisted to refloat, stood by and gave help	
	Oct.	5	Yacht *Gwynedd*, of London, saved	2
1932	Sep.	2	Fishing boat *Redwing*, of Poole, saved boat and	2
1933	Jul.	10	Motor boat *Skylark*, of Poole, gave help and landed 6	
		30	Motor yacht *Maudalric*, of London, escorted yacht to Studland Bay	
1934	Jan.	27	Canoe *Lone Star*, saved canoe and	1
	Mar.	19	Yacht *Hally Lise* (French), saved	1
	Apr.	2	Men on rocks near Old Harry, landed 2	
	Jul.	13	Small boat, of Boscombe, saved boat and	1
	Aug.	21	Man over cliffs near Old Harry Rocks, landed body	
	Oct.	22	Motor boat *Meg*, of Christchurch, saved boat and	1
1935	Apr.	21	Trawler *Norman Craig*, of Ramsgate, towed vessel and 3 to Poole	
1936	Mar.	23	Cabin cruiser, of Christchurch, towed yacht and 4 to Poole	
	Aug.	5	Steamship *Record*, of Portsmouth, towed vessel into Swanage Bay	
1937	Jul.	4	Yacht *Pauamma*, of Exeter, assisted to save yacht and	2
	Aug.	2	Yawl yacht *Bonnie Betsie*, of Weymouth, gave help	
1938	Jul.	17	Motor cruiser *Andy*, of Portsmouth, saved yacht and	2
1939	Aug.	6	Sailing dinghy *Thais*, saved dinghy	
		14	Small speed-boat, towed in boat and 1	
	Oct.	20	Steamship *Turkia*, of Piraeus, stood by	
		21	do., (second launch), stood by and gave help	
		22	do., (third launch), gave help, landed 26 and baggage	
1940	Jun.	13	Small abandoned vessel on fire, sunk by lifeboat as a danger to navigation	
	Jul.	21	Motor tanker *Kollskegg*, of Oslo, stood by and helped to connect with a tug	
	Aug.	25	German aeroplanes, salved wreckage and clothing	
1943	Dec.	21	Free French Naval vedette *Chasseur 5*, saved	3
1944	Jan.	26	Aeroplane, salved wreckage	
1945	Dec.	10	Steamship *T. A. Johnston*, of Pensacola, U.S.A., stood by	
		11	do. (second launch), stood by	
1946	Oct.	14	Barge *Monarch*, of Rochester, towed barge and 2 to Poole	
1947	Apr.	27	Motor fishing boat *Verona*, of Poole, towed vessel and 3 to Weymouth	
	Aug.	21	Motor launch *Marlene Dolores*, towed in launch	
		30	Ex-naval whaler, towed in whaler and 3	
	Sep.	2	Auxiliary sloop *Mignonette*, of Southampton, saved yacht and 4	
1948	Jul.	4	Yacht *Gadfly*, of Poole, saved yacht and	2

R.L.P. Lifeboat

1950	Apr.	16	'Vampire' aeroplane, saved	1
	Aug.	29	Motor boat and sailing dinghy, saved drifting boats	
	Sep.	3	Racing yacht, of Swanage, saved yacht and	3
1951	Nov.	4	Schooner yacht *Lamorna*, of Southampton, in tow of H.M.S. *Redpole*, stood by	
1952	Sep.	20	Motor yacht *Naiad*, of Beaumaris, towed yacht and 7 to Sandbanks	

	Oct.	1	Steam salvage vessel *Abide*, of Peterhead, saved vessel and	8
1953	Jul.	27	Rowing boat, saved boat and	2
1954	May	23	Motor boat *Dorothy*, towed boat and 2 to Swanage	
	Jul.	31	Motor yacht *Mark*, of London, towed in yacht and 2	
			Woman trapped at foot of cliff at Tillywhim, gave help	
	Sep.	10	Sloop yacht *Osterling*, of Southampton, towed in yacht and 4	

Edmund and Mary Robinson (reserve) Lifeboat

1955	Sep.	1	Auxiliary sloop yacht *Kastag*, of London, towed in yacht and 2	

R.L.P. Lifeboat

1955	Dec.	12	Barge *Sandheap*, of London, saved	1
1956	Jun.	16	Rowing boat, saved	1
	Jul.	29	Yacht *Omega*, of London, saved	4
	Aug.	11	Yacht *Melanie*, of London, saved (also a dog)	3
			Dinghy of yacht *Melanie*, saved	3
	Dec.	3	Auxiliary ketch yacht *Miss Brittany*, of Falmouth, towed yacht and 3 to Swanage	
1957	Apr.	25	Cutter yacht *Janice*, of Bosham, saved yacht and	3
	Jun.	4	Auxiliary cutter yacht *Solent Shirl*, of Southampton, saved yacht and	4
		12	Cabin cruiser *Penguin of Thelma*, saved yacht and	2
	Sep.	11	Boy over the cliff at Ballard Down, recovered body	
	Oct.	9	Cabin cruiser *William III*, of Dover, saved yacht and	1
1958	Jul.	3	Bathers near Peveril Point, saved	2
		27	Man over cliffs at Ballard Point, landed a body	
	Sep.	30	Yacht *Farida*, of Poole, saved yacht and	2
			do. (second service), saved yacht and	2
	Dec.	10	Barge *No. C.679*, stood by while derelict barge taken in tow	

Edmund and Mary Robinson (reserve) Lifeboat

1959	May	17	Four canoes, saved canoes and	5
		23	Yacht *Frolic*, of Falmouth, saved yacht and	4

R.L.P. Lifeboat

	Aug.	18	People on cliff at Ballard Point, gave help	
		31	Yacht *Shearwater*, of Poole, landed 3	
	Sep.	23	Yacht *Little Zackery*, of Hamble, saved yacht and	1
1960	Jan.	17	Persons on the cliff near Anvil Point, landed 3	
	Mar.	29	Motor vessel *Magrix*, of Hull, gave help and stood by while refloating	
	Apr.	17	Yacht *Goosander*, saved yacht and	4
			Yacht *Barbar*, towed yacht and 3 to Swanage	
	May	14	Army Sailing Association dinghies, saved two dinghies and	4
		15	Boys on the cliff at Ballard Head, gave help	
	Jun.	4	Boy over the cliff at Old Harry Rocks, landed 1 and saved	1
		8	Yacht *Periwinkle*, saved yacht and	2
	Aug.	4	Yacht *Fairwinds*, took over tow from motor vessel *Camroux I* and brought yacht and 2 to Swanage	
		14	Yacht *Maricke*, towed yacht and 2 to Poole harbour	
	Sep.	17	Fishing boat *Mary Anne*, of Poole, saved boat and	1
	Oct.	8	Sailing yacht *Pleiades*, of Guernsey, saved yacht and	3
1961	Aug.	10-11	Sailing yacht *Yangtze*, towed yacht to Swanage	
1962	Mar.	10	Motor vessel *Sand Dart*, of Southampton, saved	5
			do. (second launch) assisted in salvage operations	
	Apr.	22	Outboard motor dinghy, saved dinghy and	2

Edmund and Mary Robinson (reserve) Lifeboat

	Aug.	20	Sailing dinghy *Puffin*, towed in dinghy and 5

The Russian brigantine Otto, with flint stones, and the Dutch schooner Zwantje Cornelia, with coal, were driven on to Weymouth Sands in a gale on New Year's Day, 1912. Both were subsequently refloated.   [Photo: Eric Latcham Collection]

The self-righting lifeboat Augustus Arkwright was new when this photograph was taken at Kimmeridge in 1887. From an original photograph kindly loaned by Mr. and Mrs. Marshall of Goulter, Kimmeridge. Mrs. Marshall's father was Harry Whiterow, one of no less than six Whiterows in this crew.

The tragic wreck of the steamship Treveal *took place on Kimmeridge Ledge on the night of January 9th-10th 1920. The Weymouth lifeboat was towed to the scene in terrible weather conditions but found the wreck already abandoned. Only seven out of 43 men reached the shore alive.* [*Photo: Eric Latcham Collection*]

The ketch Diana, *disabled when her mainsail tackle broke on April 1st 1922 off Peveril Ledge, drifted ashore in Durlston Bay. The rocket apparatus saved the captain, his wife, son and crew.* [*Photo: G. F. Haysom*]

R.L.P. Lifeboat

Year	Month	Day	Description	No.
	Nov.	23	Motor fishing vessel *Lundy*, of Jersey, towed in vessel and	1
1963	Apr.	12	Outboard motor rubber dinghy, saved boat (also a dog) and	2
	Jun.	4	French yacht *Stellar*, in tow of motor fishing vessel *Purbeck Isle*, escorted vessels	
	Aug.	24	Sailing dinghy, saved dinghy	
	Oct.	13	Man over cliff at Anvil Point, landed a body	
1964	Apr.	12	Cabin cruiser *Freda Mary*, saved yacht	
	Oct.	5	Motor cruiser *Shoanne*, saved yacht and	1
	Dec.	1	Cabin cruiser, towed yacht and 2 to Weymouth	
1965	Apr.	16	Outboard motor dinghy *Sea Hawk*, saved dinghy and	2
		17	Fishing boat *Valhalla*, of Newhaven, saved boat and	3
		19	Cabin cruiser *Freeleen*, escorted to Poole Harbour	
	May	2	Yacht *Brumby*, of Portsmouth, escorted yacht to Poole	
		8	Man trapped on cliff at Warbarrow Head, saved	1
	Jun.	9	Motor vessel *Sand Star*, of Southampton, landed an injured man	
	Jul.	29	Yacht *Sea Ventures 3*, of Lymington, saved yacht and	5
	Sep.	7	Motor cruiser *Janet*, towed yacht and 3 to Swanage	
		17	Sailing dinghy of the 'Albacore' class, saved dinghy and	2
	Oct.	26	Youth fallen over the cliff near Anvil Point, landed injured man	
1966	May	15	Fishing boat *Mambo*, saved boat and	1
			Bather, saved	1
			Sailing dinghy, transferred 2 to a motor boat	
		20	Sailing dinghy, saved dinghy and	1
		22	Sailing dinghy of the 'Albacore' class, saved dinghy	
		29	Dinghy from yacht *Venturess*, of Southampton, transferred 1 to the yacht	
	Jun.	5	Sloop yacht *Sirena VII*, towed yacht and 4 to Poole	
	Aug.	14	Man over cliff at Anvil Point, landed injured man	
	Oct.	16	Skin divers, saved a rubber dinghy and	8
		22	Yacht *Sea Ventures 3*, landed 3 from motor vessel *Makefjell*, and towed in yacht	
			Motor yacht *Espadarte*, escorted to Swanage Bay	
	Nov.	5	Yacht *Blinkbonny*, of Littlehampton, saved boat and	2
	Dec.	1	Motor vessel *Maya*, of Beirut, landed a sick man	
1967	Mar.	11	Two canoes, saved canoes and	1
		26	Man in the sea at Old Harry Rocks, landed a body	
	May	3	Sailing dinghy *Faust*, saved boat and	2
		8	Bather, landed 1	
		20	Four dinghies, saved a dinghy and	4
			landed a dinghy and 4	
			escorted two dinghies and crews to shore	
	Jun.	21	Cabin cruiser *Iona*, saved yacht and	2
	Jul.	16	Yacht *Pace*, of Southampton, towed yacht and 3 to Swanage	
	Aug.	7	Motor boat, saved boat and	2
	Sep.	3	Skin divers, saved two dinghies and	4
	Oct.	6	Motor fishing vessel *Kentish Maid*, saved vessel and	2
		14	Yacht *Piccanin*, saved yacht and	2
1968	Mar.	10	Cliff climbers, saved	2
	Apr.	12	Motor boat *Shannon Mist*, of London, gave help	
	May	31	Sailing dinghy *Arne*, saved dinghy and	2
	June	2	Youth stranded on Ballard Cliff, saved	1
	July	2	Yacht *Mistra*, of Bosham, saved yacht and	4
		13	Skin divers, landed 2	
	Aug.	1	Youth on cliff, landed 1	
	Sept.	2	Boy on cliff, gave help	
		4	Yacht *Quatorze*, of Southampton, escorted yacht	
			Dinghy in tow of yacht *Sesta*, escorted boats	

	Oct.	26	Sailing dinghy, saved dinghy and	5
	Nov.	12	Yacht *Halcyon*, gave help and escorted yacht	

Rosa Woodd and Phyllis Lunn (reserve) Lifeboat

1969	Mar.	29	Girls cut off by tide at Old Harry Rocks, saved	2
	Apr.	5	Injured man at foot of cliffs, stood by during rescue from land	
			Sloop *Compass Rose*, gave help	
	May	11	Three persons on rocks, gave help	
		16	Person fallen from cliff, stood by during rescue	
	June	8	Woman stranded on cliff, landed injured woman	

R.L.P. Lifeboat

	June	14	Cabin cruiser *Mariposa*, gave help	
		18	Sailing dinghy, assisted to save (also landed a body)	2
		21	Yacht *Lydos*, saved yacht and	2
	July	6	Catamaran *Vaapit*, saved yacht and	2
		7	Dinghy *Mary Jane*, saved boat and	3
		13	Motor cruiser *Right Narna*, of Poole, gave help	
		23	Boys on cliff, landed 2	
		30	Dinghy in tow of yacht *Bobolink*, gave help and landed 4	
	Aug.	20	Men stranded on cliff at Ballard Head, saved injured man	1
			do. (second service), landed police cliff rescue team and second rescued man	
		23	Yacht *Luran*, saved yacht and	2
		28	Yacht *Havorn*, saved yacht and	2
	Sept.	2	Fishing boat *We'll Try*, gave help	
			Trimaran *Suedor*, of Poole, saved yacht and	4
		6	Girl trapped on cliff, gave help	
	Oct.	6	Man stranded on cliffs, assisted to save	1
		26	Yacht *Argo of Arne*, gave help	
1970	Jan.	23	Motor vessel *Albert*, of Bremen, gave help	
	Feb.	28	Fishing vessel *Bon Adventure*, of Weymouth, gave help	
	Apr.	5	Yacht *Gemini* and skin divers, saved yacht and	5
			Sailing dinghy, gave help	
		12	Sailing dinghy, gave help and landed 1	
		19	Girl fallen over cliff, gave help	
		25	Sailing dinghies, saved 2 boats and	3
		30	Motor vessel *Lumey*, of Groningen (Netherlands), stood by	

5

STUDLAND and POOLE

THE SOMEWHAT OBSCURE Studland Bay lifeboat station is advisedly linked with Poole since its function was to protect the outer anchorage and entrance to that ancient port. The bay has always been the roadstead for Poole in spite of its position exposed to easterly and southerly winds, and its dangers such as the Milkmaid Shoal and the shifting Hook Sands. Ashore as well as below water, the contours are constantly changing, and the peninsula known as Sandbanks is being built up with sand eroded from the east—to Bournemouth's dismay.

At or near Studland an Armada ship was wrecked. She was the *San Salvador* which Laird Clowes describes as of 958 tons and 25 guns, having on board 321 soldiers and 75 seamen—in what conditions one hesitates to contemplate. She was one of the Armada of Guipuzcoa, under Miguel de Oquendo, and was captured somewhere in mid-channel but lost when being taken back to Weymouth as prize.

A couple of hundred years later *Lloyd's List* frequently named casualties in the area. In March 1788, the *Fame*, bound for Newfoundland 'got ashore going out of the harbour and bulged'. In December 1788 the *Nautilous* (*sic*) bound for Bilbao, was 'ashore near Pool harbour; hope will get off next Springs by lightening'. In February 1790, the *Providence*, 'from Leverpool, ashore on the Hook Sands; feared will be lost'. In February 1799, the *Eagle* gunboat and cutter of about 50 tons 'drove ashore in a violent gale of wind, in Studland Bay'. A few days later the *Bee*, an outward-bound London West-Indiaman, which had probably sought shelter from a westerly gale, went ashore near Poole—'expect to save cargo', the earliest specialised newspaper said succinctly. In November 1810 the *Dove*, of Southampton, was 'a total loss in Studland Roads on the 10th, and all hands'. These are but a sample of many in similar vein extending over the best part of a century.

Clearly there was need for a lifeboat somewhere just outside Poole Harbour and Studland was the best site if one considered the wind was most often westerly. Here there would be the protection afforded by the high ground to the west for sheltered launching and also a community of fishermen, pilots and others to supply the crew. We have noted in the introductory chapter that the Dorset Life-saving Association, with the co-operation of the parent society in London, placed its first lifeboat at Portland and considered a second for Abbotsbury. In the event, however, the second went to Studland in May or June 1826. It is possible that the timely casualty which suggested the suitability of Studland was the *Lark*, a small vessel of Christchurch, from which two men were saved by the exertions of Lieutenant Joseph Elwin, R.N., and two of his Coastguards. Elwin was awarded the silver medal of the Institution. Unfortunately the records do not mention the date of the casualty—it was either in December 1824 or early in January 1825—judging by the date of the award. Moreover the difficulties in interpreting some of these early reports are exemplified by the entry concerning this vessel. The rescue was said to have been at 'Flag Head, Branksea Island, near Lymington'. Flag Head does not now exist but, also known as Poole Head, it was the high sandy cliff at the base of the narrow spit which runs out to Sandbanks. Its name is perpetuated in Flag Head Chine. It seems also to have been the name if not the actual site of the old Coastguard Station, recorded as having a Manby mortar for life-saving purposes from about 1824. Then Branksea Island is within the harbour, so there is ambiguity as to the actual location of the casualty. The 'near Lymington' is also puzzling, but a likely explanation is that Lymington was at the time the headquarters of the Coastguard district—bearing in mind that at that period the reports sent in by Coastguard officers were used to decide which rescues should be rewarded.

The Studland lifeboat was of the type designed by Pellew Plenty, of Newbury in Berkshire; 20 ft. long and pulling six or eight oars. She was kept on a carriage in a boat-house 30 yards from high water mark and, sad to say, was virtually forgotten. In 1848, in response to an inquiry by the Institution the Chief Officer of Coastguards reported that she had never been used to save life and was now decayed and unfit. An Inspector's survey in 1850 confirmed her useless condition and, it having been ascertained she could not be repaired economically, she was put up for sale in March 1852.

Oddly enough Studland Bay appears only once in the *Annual Reports* of the parent Institution between the *Lark* rescue of 1824-5, and the establishment of the Poole lifeboat station in 1865. This was the rescue early in January 1837, of two men from a canoe, by one Thomas Cook, singlehanded in his boat. For this he received a sovereign, the usual reward, but we must bear in mind that it would represent some £10 of our money today.

There were other early rescues in the eastern part of the area now covered by the Poole lifeboat, but strictly they belong to the wreck history of Hampshire. They include the very first award of a R.N.I.P.L.S gold medal—to Captain C. W. Fremantle, R.N., for his attempt to rescue the crew of a Swedish brig wrecked at Christchurch in 1824. The gallant captain swam with a line to the wreck, but the endangered crew could not be persuaded to follow his directions. The wreck then beginning to break up, the Captain narrowly escaped with his own life, being hauled ashore by his line, exhausted and insensible. The brig's crew later got away along one of her masts which luckily fell shorewards. There was also the wreck of the *Hero*, of Southampton, at Christchurch Head later in the same year when George Barnes and Stephen Curtis won silver medals.

Rather later, on December 27th 1852, there was a memorable rescue by Coastguards in their galley of eight men from the barque *William Glen Anderson*, of Poole, from Quebec, which drove ashore at Boscombe in a southerly gale. This earned the silver medal for Lieutenant Parsons, R.N., Chief Officer of Bournebottom Coastguard station, who coxed the galley, rowed by four of his men. On the same occasion they saved four of five men from a lifeboat belonging to Sir Percy Shelley's yacht which had put off to help but had capsized.

No single wreck is recorded as having brought about the foundation of the Poole station and it was probably the result of a series of strandings of incoming and outgoing vessels such as was noted earlier. Harry Matthews, in one of his newspaper articles, says that the Reverend Lord Osborn and the quaker George Penny were the prime movers in petitioning the Institution. The lifeboat house was built at North Haven Point, now more familiarly known as Sandbanks, so that the boat could be launched inside or outside the harbour as required. As can be imagined the point was then a remote outpost frequented mainly by Coastguards and fishermen. There was at least one fisherman's cottage, for the intrepid Richard Sutton Stokes, who was appointed the first coxswain, was born there and coupled his trade as pilot with looking after the primitive leading lights which Trinity House had established in about 1848 at the harbour entrance. The rest of the lifeboat crew had to be brought by horse brake from Poole, the assembly point being the Antelope Inn in High Street.

The house, described as 'very commodious and substantial', cost

£252 and was built on a plot of land given by Sir William Guest. The first boat, the *Manley Wood*, of the 32-feet ten-oared self-righting class, and its carriage, were the gift of an anonymous lady. There was a 'grand demonstration' at Poole on January 19th 1865, when the equipage arrived via the London and South Western Railway and was ceremonially christened on the Quay.

The first service launch of the *Manley Wood* came just over a year later, on February 11th 1866, when she went out in a terrific south-easterly gale, towed by Miss Charlotte Fayle's wooden paddle tug *Royal Albert*—Poole harbour's work-horse of those days. Unfortunately, in the words of the contemporary report, she 'could render no assistance' to an unknown vessel reported in distress in Studland Bay. Later on the same day there was a further call to the brigantine *Elizabeth*, of Exeter, ashore on Christchurch Bar. It was decided to take the lifeboat by road to Christchurch, but she was not in fact launched. First success came a year later when, on January 8th 1867, they went out to the brig *Antares*, of Grieffswald in Prussia, with a cargo of cork from Portugal, ashore on the Hook Sands at the entrance to the harbour. The *Manley Wood* brought the master ashore to arrange for a tug, then returning to the brig to stand by until she had been towed in.

In the following November, there was a series of launches to the Guernsey brig *Contest*. On the 16th the brig went aground on the Hook Sands in a bitter easterly gale, but when the lifeboat came alongside her crew would not leave. Coxswain Stokes decided to stand by in case of need and they were there for three hours, the men suffering greatly without shelter in the open boat, and returned to Poole only when the brig was left steady by the falling tide so that the danger was past for the time being. A second launch on the next tide had the same result, and the lifeboat returned after arranging a signal to be made if help was required. During the day 36 labourers were put on board the *Contest* to lighten her by throwing overboard some of her granite cargo. Some time later the prearranged signal was made and the lifeboat went out, towed by the *Royal Albert*. She first took a warp from the tug to the brig but in a short while it broke. The brig's master then signalled that he would abandon ship. The tug towed the lifeboat to and fro three times, on the first trip taking off and landing twelve. On the second, with 24 on board, the lifeboat was struck by heavy seas on the bar and was completely submerged, but she freed herself of water and landed the men, soaked but safe. A third trip brought ashore the remaining ten men, the crew of the brig, with most of their kit.

Another fine rescue was made in the following year on December 15th 1868, when, in a heavy gale from the S.S.E., two small French vessels struck the sands, one on either side of the entrance. It was reported that they had mistaken Poole for Portsmouth, whither they were bound, but this is difficult to believe in view of the very different surroundings of the two ports. With perseverance the lifeboat crew got the lugger *Augustine*, of Pont L'Abbé, afloat and brought her and her crew of four into the harbour. Going to the second vessel, the *Jeune Erneste*, of Bordeaux, they found her abandoned and full of water.

Several years passed and not until March 12th 1876 did the *Manley Wood* add another service to the record. She went off in a strong southwesterly gale to a vessel reported ashore to the east. She found the small local ketch *William Pitt* ashore near Bournemouth Pier, surrounded by surf extending a long way from the shore. Only one man was on board and he was saved, the lifeboat crew being glad to accept a tow back to Poole by the ever ready *Royal Albert*.

The last service of this first Poole lifeboat was performed on March 27th 1879, when the iron full-rigged ship *Martaban*, of Greenock, stranded on the Hook Sands in the night. Going off at about two in the morning they found that six of the ship's crew had left in one of their own boats. When the lifeboat had stood by for eleven hours the *Martaban*'s master decided he would abandon ship, and the remaining eleven men were taken off and landed at Poole. The ship was later refloated and brought into the harbour for repairs.

At about this time the services of the tug were placed on a regular footing and a fee of £5 was agreed for each service on which the *Royal Albert* was employed.

In 1879 the *Manley Wood* was appropriated to the legacy of Mrs. Boetefeur of London and renamed *Joseph and Mary*, but she had no further service launches. In 1880 a new, slightly larger, ten-oared lifeboat was sent to Poole also named *Joseph and Mary*, and she in turn was renamed two years later when she was appropriated to the fund raised by readers of *Boy's Own Paper* through their popular editor G. A. Hutchison. She was named *Boy's Own No. 2*, the *No. 1* boat being sent to Looe in Cornwall. The year 1882 was also noteworthy, for in that year the lifeboat was rehoused at the south end of East Quay at Poole, the arrangement for towage making it unnecessary to continue the inconvenience and time consuming road journey to Sandbanks. The new house cost £165, but there is some evidence that it was a rebuilding of an existing boathouse rather than a completely new construction. Coxswain Richard Stokes, who had been in charge since the station opened, and helped to save 63 lives, retired in March. His duties at Sandbanks in connection with the lights probably precluded his remaining an officer of the lifeboat now it was moved. He was awarded the R.N.L.I. silver medal in recognition of his long and gallant service. This practice has long since died out and medals are now awarded only for actual acts of gallantry. One cannot help thinking that a long service medal might be a worthwhile addition to the awards.

The first service of the new lifeboat came after her renaming, although before the actual naming ceremony on July 27th. On June 1st 1882, the Swedish brigantine *Otto*, inward bound from Gefle with timber, ran on to the Milkmaid Shoal. She had been in tow, but in a strong easterly wind with heavy seas, the rope parted and she drove rapidly to leeward. She bumped heavily on the shoal and lost her rudder. Two tugs failed to refloat her and she gradually drove farther on to the shoal in the midst of breaking seas. The crew stayed on board until the wind veered southerly and increased, causing her to roll and bump even more heavily. At about midnight the *Boy's Own No.* 2 reached her and saved the crew of nine.

Just over six months later, on the afternoon of January 9th 1883, the lifeboat was towed out in a heavy gale from the E.S.E. in response to signal guns from Studland Bay. They found the large German brig *Victor*, with a coal cargo from South Wales, for her home port of Neustadt, riding in a very dangerous position. She had been damaged by the seas as she came up the Channel and had lost her figurehead as well as parts of her bow bulwarks. Seas were making a clean breach over her as she tugged at her anchor chains, but her crew would not leave. Then, by good fortune, after the lifeboat had stood by an hour or so, the weather moderated and almost at once the danger was past.

After the *Victor* service there was a gap of eight years before the next, and in the meanwhile the *Boy's Own No.* 2 was taken away to be brought up-to-date by the fitting of a drop-keel in order to improve her sailing powers. On October 26th 1891, she stood by the Plymouth schooner *Mountblairy*, which had stranded on the Hook Sands in misty weather. A heavy ground swell caused the schooner to strike the ground heavily, but the flowing tide freed her and a tug towed her back to Poole. This schooner was helped by lifeboats on several occasions until her wreck in October 1929, on the Irish coast, which was itself the occasion of an epic rescue.

Two daring rescues followed only a fortnight or so after the *Mount-*

blairy case. On November 11th, very early in the morning, the lifeboat went out in a heavy gale from the S.S.E. after signals had been heard from Studland Bay. They found the Norwegian brig *Solertia* with a cargo of Russian timber for Poole had stranded and was bumping heavily, in fact her mainmast was lying overside having been jerked right out of its 'partners'. Seas were breaking right over her and under deck she was full of water. It took five hours of manoeuvring to rescue the crew of eight and a customs officer, rescued and rescuers—exhausted alike—arriving back at Poole about 9.30 in the morning.

The rescue from the *Brilliant* has been touched upon in the Swanage chapter as it was the occasion of the tragic loss of their Coxswain. It was on the late evening of January 12th 1895, that this Norwegian barque, laden with cedar logs from Nuevitas in Cuba, bound for Bremen, went aground on the Hook Sands. A heavy force-10 gale was blowing from the S.E. by E., laced with snow, and with very heavy seas. The local steam tug *Telegraph*—another old wooden-hulled paddler—towed the *Boy's Own No. 2* to the bar and there the coxswain asked to be slipped so that they could approach the casualty with the greater manoeuvrability afforded by the oarsmen. The wreck was too exposed for the lifeboat to tie up alongside and each man had to be taken off in a fresh approach. The ship's boy broke a leg when he became entangled in a rope, but quick thinking by one of the lifeboatmen who cut the rope free saved the limb from being torn off. Captain Bjercke, who had earlier broken a rib when thrown to the deck by a wave, lost his grip on a rope and fell into the water but was quickly recovered. Eventually the whole ten were in the lifeboat and the tug passed a hawser to tow them back to Poole. This was done through a blinding snowstorm while all hands sought what comfort they could under sails folded to make a temporary shelter.

The last service of the *Boy's Own No. 2* came on February 23rd 1896, when the barquentine *Albert T. Young* and the brigantine *Hildred*, both of Faversham and both coal-laden, stranded on the back of the Hook Sands in a fresh south-easterly wind and rough seas. Labourers were taken out to lighten them and during the day there was no immediate danger. In the evening when these men were brought back in a tug, a signal was arranged between the two masters and the watchman at Sandbanks for calling out the lifeboat if necessary. The signal was shown at 9.15 p.m. and the lifeboat went off. The *Hildred*'s crew of eight would not leave, but the master of the *Albert T. Young* wanted six of his men taken ashore while he and the mate remained on board.

He wanted the lifeboat to return and stand by, and this was done all through a bitterly cold night.

Later in 1896 the *Boy's Own No. 2* was surveyed, found unfit, and at once sold. A reserve lifeboat was sent to the station and on January 23rd 1897, added a service to the record by landing two people from the local steam launch *Zulu* which was anchored in Studland Bay while rising winds and seas threatened to throw her ashore.

In March 1897 the Poole crew were asked to try one of the early Watson craft. This particular boat had had an interesting history. She had been designed by the famous naval architect George L. Watson to take part in trials of rowing lifeboats at Montrose in Scotland early in 1893. As the original Watson designed lifeboat had been stationed at Southport, this class was for some time known as the 'Southport', but later they were named after their designer. When the trials were finished this lifeboat went to Blackpool for a few months and was subsequently tried at several stations. The Poole crew liked her very much and asked if they could keep her. The Institution agreed, but it meant a change in procedure at Poole in that the 38-feet twelve-oared boat was not suitable for carriage launching. Alterations had to be made to the house and a launching slipway built. The Watson-type is not self-righting, but designed to be much steadier than the self-righters, the Poole boat also having four water-ballast tanks and a drop keel to help when sailing. Although bearing the name *City Masonic Club* since she was built, she was not ceremonially appropriated to the gift of the Freemasons until August 26th 1897. The day was marred by heavy rain, but the visiting masons in their full regalia held a public meeting in the Guildhall with Lord Wimborne, the Mayor of Poole, in the chair. They afterwards went to the boat house where Lady Wimborne formally named the boat.

The new lifeboat's first services came in that crowded three days November 23-25th 1898 when, as mentioned in the previous chapter, the *William Erle*, of Swanage, was also involved. At the finish the *City Masonic Club* had been launched five times, the veteran Coxswain John Hughes—over seventy years of age—being on duty about 48 hours, and the *William Erle* three times, on two of them with a Poole crew. The Swanage service to the *Velocity* has already been described. The Poole lifeboat twice went out to the same vessel, on the first occasion returning when the Swanage lifeboat was seen in attendance, and on the second occasion, in the evening, going with a view to relieving their colleagues. but found the distressed crew had already been taken off. She was, however, able to help by transferring one of her crew to the Swanage boat in order to pilot them to Poole Quay. Early on the following day the *City Masonic Club* went out again to the Norwegian three-masted schooner *Frier* in trouble on the Hook Sand. There was still a strong gale and heavy seas in the bay but they persevered and rescued the *Frier*'s crew of eight, the schooner afterwards driving on to the beach near Flag Head Chine. She was written off as a wreck, but was salved and repaired by a Poole man. Almost five years later to the day, on November 23rd 1903, while bound from Antwerp for Newcastle, she was blown off course by a North Sea gale and wrecked on Terschelling Sands.

We have already told how the Swanage lifeboat was taken out by a Poole crew to the French barque *Bonne Mère* and how the Poole lifeboat, after the *Frier* service, went out again to help. Both lifeboats returned to Poole in the evening of the 24th, but on the following morning the Poole boat was launched for the fifth time, again going to the *Bonne Mère*. She was able to take a hawser to a tug and, the Frenchman's anchors having been raised, she was towed to Southampton with the lifeboat towing astern in case of need. This was the longest passage undertaken by any Poole lifeboat on duty.

By comparison the later rescues of the *City Masonic Club* were unspectacular. In 1900 she stood by the inward bound steam collier *Matin* while that vessel refloated herself from the Hook Sands and found a safer anchorage. In 1902 the same sands claimed another victim, the ketch *Little Jessie*, inward bound with Lincolnshire potatoes. Called out by the Sandbanks Coastguard, the lifeboat found her striking heavily. Fortunately the tide was rising and after a while the ketch floated free and made for Poole.

In 1904 there were yet more strandings on the Hook Sands. The *City Masonic Club* was launched early on the morning of December 4th and found the schooner *Carrie Bell*, inward bound with limestone. After they stood by for some hours the schooner floated clear on the rising tide and was able to enter the harbour. The lifeboat then saw the ketch *Zenobia* ashore on the opposite side of the sands and offered help, but this was declined. As the ketch was in a dangerous position the lifeboat returned to the scene in the afternoon and in worsening weather put some men on board. By laying out kedge anchors the ketch was eventually saved.

On the morning of October 21st 1908, the Bridgwater ketch *Conquest*, outward bound for Cardiff with wheat, was towed to sea by a tug, but encountering a strong south-easterly gale and heavy seas in Studland Bay, her master signalled that he wished to return to harbour. Unfortunately while they were turning the tow rope parted and the ketch was rapidly driven on to the sands. It would have been suicidal for the tug to go alongside in the broken water and she had to stand by helplessly. The Coastguard told the lifeboat authorities and the *City Masonic Club* came out. Eight lifeboatmen were put on board to pump, and with the lifeboat in attendance, they worked for five hours, but unfortunately to no avail for the ketch had sustained severe damage under water. She refused to float with the tide and it became obvious she would break up. Her crew of four and pilot were rescued, all suffering severely from cold and exposure.

The *City Masonic Club* performed her last service on the evening of January 11th 1910, when fourteen local fishing boats were caught at sea by a sudden gale. Many of the lifeboatmen were in them and a scratch crew of veterans had to be mustered. They took the lifeboat to the harbour entrance where there was a mass of broken water caused by the gale and the racing currents, and there stood by in case of trouble. Their presence greatly encouraged the fishermen and all got to safety with some damage and some narrow escapes.

In May 1910, a new self-righting lifeboat of the latest type, 37½-feet long, with twelve oars and two drop-keels, was sent to Poole. She was named *Harmar*, being the gift of the late George John Harmar, of Kensington. Miss Daisy Harmar formally named the lifeboat on June 4th, having to make a quick move when the accidental firing of the launching maroon cut short the Mayor's speech and the launchers knocked out the pin which held the boat at the head of the slip.

The *Harmar* had a most successful career of 29 years and saved sixty lives. Her first service came on December 19th 1913, when she saved the London barge *Emma and John* and her crew of two. Inward bound with linseed cake from London, the barge was driven on the Hook Sands in an easterly gale. The obvious first course was to remove the crew, but later it became evident the barge had withstood the pounding on the sands without serious damage. At the first opportunity the crew were reboarded with three lifeboatmen, and after a spell at the pumps they refloated the barge with the rising tide and sailed her into the safety of the harbour.

After two more services to vessels on the Hook Sands there was a war service on November 13th 1915, when the crew of ten was saved from the naval trawler *King Heron*. Signals of distress had been seen from near the Old Harry Rocks, and going out soon after four in the morning, they found the trawler stranded on the Old Harry Ledge. A first attempt to reach them failed owing to the strong tide and heavy sea, so the lifeboat was headed to sea again to try another approach. Another naval trawler came to the scene and towed the *Harmar* to windward, from which position she could veer down and save the men. Afterwards the other trawler towed the lifeboat back to Poole Harbour.

Almost a year later, on October 22nd 1916, they rescued the crew of seven of another of the Navy's maids-of-all-work, the drifter *Fame*, wrecked on the Hook Sands in a south-easterly gale. Then on March 3rd 1917, the *Harmar* was able to help in saving one of the small sailing coasters which still had a part to play at the time of the first world war. The ketch *Boaz* was bound from Poole for Caen, with ironwork, when she stranded on the Hook in a strong easterly breeze. The lifeboat was able to take a hawser to a tug, and after a while the *Boaz* was eased out of her sandy bed and towed clear.

In 1917 it was decided to rename the station Poole and Bournemouth in order to forge a closer link between the two adjoining towns. However they subsequently reverted to separate committees and in 1953 the lifeboat station again became known as Poole.

It was during the post-war clearing-up operations, when numbers of captured and obsolete warships were being towed to various places for breaking up, that the *Harmar* had the opportunity to perform her finest service. Early on the morning of January 8th 1919, the surrendered German submarine *U.143* grounded on the Hook Sands during a whole southerly gale, and as daylight came she was seen surrounded by broken water with the seas frequently sweeping right over her. She had been on her way to Japan as an item of war reparations, escorted by the Japanese destroyers *Kanran* and *Kashiwa*, but had approached the coast for shelter as her engines were giving trouble. The destroyers could not approach the sands owing to their deep draught and the British naval drifter *White Oak*, called from Portland to assist, also could not get close enough. After exchanges of wireless messages Portland naval base asked for the services of the Poole lifeboat and at about eleven o'clock the *White Oak* entered the harbour to tow the *Harmar* to the scene. The tide was almost full again and the *U.143* was lifting slightly, but the seas were still sweeping over the bank with great force. The senior Japanese naval officer asked the Coxswain to take wires to the submarine and to pass them to the tug *Commerce* which had come to help. However in spite of continual towing the peak of the tide passed without any improvement in the submarine's position. The drifter was then employed passing stronger wires from the destroyers so that a further attempt could be made on the night tide. The Japanese crew refused to abandon ship without orders so the men in the *Harmar* settled down for a long vigil as they rolled and tossed at the end of their anchor chain in the lee of the *Kanran*. They had been out there nearly twelve hours, wet and frozen, when the darkness was lit by the flash of distress rockets to the west. Quickly heaving in their cable and setting reefed sails they broke out their anchor and made for the new casualty. She was found to be the steel motor schooner *Zwaluw*, of Antwerp, which was dragging her anchors shorewards. Her master asked for a lifeboatman as a pilot and one went on board, but in spite of all possible manoeuvres they could not wear away from the land and were eventually driven aground close to the shore. With great difficulty, striking the bottom in the troughs of the breakers, the lifeboat got alongside, took off the crew of nine, and landed them at Poole at 3.30 on the morning of the 9th. Six hours later, refreshed, slightly rested and in dry clothes, the crew assembled to go out again to the submarine. She was found to have remained fast and her crew to be safe for the time being, so the lifeboat was brought back. During the day the Japanese crew received orders by wireless to abandon ship, and a message was sent to the lifeboat secretary. The *Harmar* went out for a third time at 5.30 in the afternoon, and in two trips transferred the crew of 28 to the destroyer, which was now anchored within the harbour. The Royal Navy drifter assisted by towing the lifeboat to and from the harbour entrance on each trip. A week or so later tugs managed to refloat the submarine, more or less undamaged.

Shortly before noon on April 21st 1921, the *Harmar* went out to Christchurch Ledge where the Belgian collier *Fernande*, bound for Portland, had earlier stranded in foggy weather. A south-westerly wind had blown away the fog and showed the steamer in a dangerous position, rolling and bumping in a strong swell. Her master asked them to stand by until the next tide, and she was then refloated by the efforts of two tugs and her own engines. The *Harmar* escorted tugs and tow to Portland.

Subsequent services of the *Harmar* were generally cases of standing by vessels ashore on the Hook Sands or the shores near the harbour entrance. Many of the vessels had been sheltering windbound, and in most cases survived their mishaps. The *Sidney*, on October 15th 1922, was from Guernsey with broken granite and was stranded off the shore to the west of the harbour entrance. She was towed off undamaged. The *Pioneer*, a fortnight later, was inward bound with general cargo from the Channel Islands and caught fire when at the mouth of the harbour. She was helped into shallow water and beached, the fire being subdued in a short while.

In 1931 the barge *Genesta*, inward bound without cargo, broke her sprit and became unmanageable. She anchored to avoid going ashore near Sandbanks, and lifeboatmen helped her crew of two to raise the anchor so that she could be towed into the harbour by a motor vessel.

Of the last services of the *Harmar*, that to the London collier *Pitwines* involved standing by through the night of November 13-14th 1932, and in the morning taking lines to a tug by which she was eventually refloated. She was ashore west of the bar buoy in a dangerous position. The crew of two of the small yacht *Glencora* had a narrow escape. Powered by an auxiliary motor they were coming from Southampton when they ran on to the training bank outside the harbour entrance. The weather was thick and it was very dark. The boat was holed on a boulder, heeled over and sank. They lit a signal flare and climbed the mast to get out of reach of the waves. Local pilots, thinking the signal was for their services, went out in a motor boat and, sizing up the situation, tried to get alongside to take off the men but after being nearly swamped, were frustrated by the heavy surf breaking on the bank. They returned to the harbour and informed the lifeboat authorities. They also made contact with the Harbour Master (Commander Euman, R.N.), and his motor launch was made available to tow the lifeboat to the scene, so saving considerable time. By then the hull of the yacht was submerged, and the two men were taken from the rigging with great difficulty owing both to the heavy seas and their own exhausted condition.

On the night of September 16-17th 1935, there was a severe southwesterly gale in the Poole area and forty craft of all sizes were broken from their moorings. Five of these sank, and high tides left many small boats on the quays and the harbour banks, far above normal high water mark. The large Bermudian cutter yacht *Foxhound*, only two months old, broke adrift from her two anchors in the harbour. Her two hands lit a flare and the lifeboat was launched. Unfortunately the yacht drifted among intricate channels in the mud and in approaching the lifeboat herself went aground. It was obvious she would not refloat until the next tide. Six men then put off in a rowing boat and with their lighter draught could take off the yacht hands, although not without danger from the swift flowing currents. The lifeboat was refloated on the 18th, undamaged save for a torn mainsail.

A few days later, on September 28th, the *Harmar* went off to a converted ship's lifeboat with four men which had stranded outside the harbour. They stood by until the tide floated the boat and then towed her to Poole. Just under three years later, on June 1st 1938, the *Harmar* landed a man from the yacht *Zaire* moored in the harbour during a gale from the W.S.W., and this ended the sailing lifeboat era at this station. The *Harmar* had seen forty service launches and saved sixty lives.

The motor lifeboat *Thomas Kirk Wright* arrived on January 12th 1939, one of the light 'Surf' type, only 32 feet long and so in fact smaller than her predecessor, but with the far greater potential afforded by motor power. She had two twelve horse-power engines driving Hotchkiss internal cone propellers, an arrangement giving great manoeuvrability while retaining the advantages of drawing less water than would be possible with conventional screws. The boat was divided into three watertight compartments and had 83 air-cases, a watertight engine-room and automatic water-freeing ports. She could travel 44 miles without refuelling and could take fifteen men on board in rough weather. She was thus not really a deep-sea lifeboat, but well able to cope with casualties in Studland Bay and to the east as far as Christchurch. She was a local gift, being provided from part of the legacy of T. H. Kirk Wright, of Bournemouth.

The inaugural ceremony was on June 7th 1939, but she had by then already marked up her maiden service. Quite soon after her arrival on station, at about noon on January 22nd, information was received that the local motor launch *Snapper*, bound for Southampton, was in trouble off Boscombe Pier in a rough sea. The launch had been towing a dinghy and two of her crew of three used this to reach the pier. The lifeboat put another man on board and towed the launch back to Poole.

The only completed service of the war period at Poole began with a launch moments after midnight early on January 1st 1940, after the Coastguard had reported a boat ashore on Christchurch Bar, but not in immediate danger. The night was dark and foggy and there was a moderate easterly wind. They found the cabin cruiser *Sea Mist* leaking badly. Her crew had attempted to get away in their dinghy but it had been swamped. Two of them were taken into the lifeboat and two lifeboatmen put on the yacht, which was then towed to a safe berth in Christchurch Harbour.

Five months later, on May 30th, a brief crowded interlude began

The crew of the Swanage lifeboat Herbert Sturmy *in 1924, with the signalman and station officers.* [*Photo: R.N.L.I.*]

The present motor lifeboat at Swanage is the R.L.P., *a 41 ft. Watson-class craft, built in 1949. She is seen here after being fitted with new diesel engines and having other improvements in 1962.*

The first Poole lifeboat Manley Wood, *which was stationed at Sandbanks from 1865 to 1880, a 32 ft., ten-oared self-righting boat. She saved 63 lives while commanded by the famous Coxswain Richard Stokes who is seen standing at the stern.*

[*Photo: R.N.L.I.*]

An early Watson-type sailing lifeboat, the City Masonic Club, *which was stationed at Poole between 1897 and 1910. She was 38 ft. long and had a crew of 15.*

[*Photo: R.N.L.I.*]

when, in response to calls for small craft to rendezvous with a view to the evacuation of our troops from the Dunkirk area, the naval-officer-in-charge at Poole commandeered the *Thomas Kirk Wright*, and at once sent her to Dover. She was thus the first lifeboat taken over for the purpose, but on that same day the R.N.L.I. were asked to send others, and in all nineteen took part in the operation. At Dunkirk the Poole lifeboat was used to ferry troops from the beaches to waiting warships, but the combination of arduous work in shallow sandy water and of being handled by personnel unused to her system of propulsion led to one of her motors being put out of action. She was lucky not to be abandoned at the scene and was towed back to Dover where she was repaired when the great operation had been finished.

The rest of the war passed with several calls such as on June 12th 1940, when the Dutch motor coasting vessel *Prinses Juliana* was mined, but the pilot boat was at hand to pick up the survivors, and on July 18th 1940, when an aircraft crashed into the sea, but the pilot was picked up by another boat before the lifeboat arrived.

After the war the south coast, from being an armed camp and in-vasion base, turned back to peacetime pursuits as soon as possible. The season of 1946 saw a few paddle steamers and trip-boats plying from the resorts. Unfortunately there was a mishap on the afternoon of April 21st when the motor boat *Skylark* sprang a leak and sank off Alum Chine while taking about seventy visitors on a cruise round Bourne-mouth Bay. Luckily the weather was fine and the sea smooth, for there were the makings of catastrophe. Boats quickly put off from nearby beaches, including two which were each manned by a schoolboy. One aged 14, and the other, aged 15, each saved five lives. The police told the Poole lifeboat authorities, but having five miles to cover, the *Thomas Kirk Wright* arrived to find the rescue work almost completed. How-ever she did find one man drifting to sea on a raft. He was rescued and put aboard one of the other boats returning to Bournemouth Pier. One crew member of the *Skylark* died.

Apart from a case on September 17th 1947, when wreckage from a crashed 'Spitfire' was recovered, every subsequent service at Poole, save one, has been to some form of pleasure craft. It suffices here to deal only with a representative few, the remainder being listed at the end of the chapter.

On the evening of October 7th 1953, the cutter yacht *Freda*, on pas-sage from Hamble, struck the boulders of the training bank outside Poole harbour and remained aground. Four persons were on board and they burnt flares which gave rise to an erroneous report that she was on fire. However the lifeboat was launched in five minutes from receiving the report and went out in a moderate breeze from the E.N.E. and ground swell. The falling tide had left the yacht on her side, but she was fairly buoyant and after four attempts the lifeboat refloated her and towed her to Poole.

Early on the morning of May 29th 1957, the Coastguard reported a small yacht aground off Sandbanks. The tide was low as the lifeboat came to the scene and found the yacht *Brief Encounter*, of Southampton, with a crew of two. The second coxswain was put on board to help, and the lifeboat stood by until the rising tide floated the yacht which was then towed into the harbour. On November 30th following, the lifeboat stood by the Netherlands motor vessel *Dollard* aground on the Hook Sands. After about three hours the rising tide refloated the coaster without damage.

The *Thomas Kirk Wright* was replaced in 1962 by the slightly larger 'Liverpool' type lifeboat *Bassett Green* which, since 1951, had been the Padstow No. 2 lifeboat and had there been launched thirteen times and saved six lives[1]. At Poole it was decided that as the small fishermen's harbour, into which the lifeboats had hitherto been launched, was subject to serious silting, the *Bassett Green* would be kept afloat just off the lifeboat house, and boarded by means of a small boat kept ready at all times.

The new lifeboat was called out for the first time at Poole in the late afternoon of August 14th 1962, to a small yacht in difficulties off the Hook Sands in a strong south-easterly breeze and rough seas. She was at the scene in 25 minutes and in that short time the wind had veered to south-west and moderated. It was necessary only to escort the yacht, with her crew of two, to a safe anchorage. In September she had a long twelve hours on two missions searching the harbour for missing craft in a south-easterly gale. At nine on the evening of the 29th a man and a baby were reported missing in the yacht *Margara Della*. The yacht had run aground and a passing boat had taken the man's wife ashore to seek help. The lifeboat found that after drifting a while on the flood tide the man had successfully anchored. With the baby he was taken to Poole Quay, arriving soon after eleven. Just over three hours later, at 2.35 a.m. on the 30th, the Coastguard reported two men missing in the cabin cruiser *Sea Knight*, after having put out the previous day to dig for

1 See *Wreck and Rescue Round the Cornish Coast*, vol. I, pp. 78-81.

bait at Goathorn. The lifeboat found the yacht ashore at Furzey Island, but the men were missing. Some lifeboatmen searched the small island without result. The lifeboat was still searching when a radio message was received through Niton that the men had been landed at Sandbanks by a boatman. They then refloated the *Sea Knight* and took her to safe moorings, arriving back on station at 10.15 in the morning.

In 1963, in view of the number of calls which were being made to casulties within the harbour, where a smaller rescue craft would be sufficient and indeed an advantage when the shallows had to be crossed a 12-feet rubber rowing dinghy was provided for carrying by the lifeboat when necessary. In the following year this dinghy was fitted with an outboard motor. This was used to advantage on May 1st 1964, when she was called out to a capsized speed-boat, but in fact no service resulted. The call was at about 10.45 in the evening after cries for help had been heard coming from the harbour. A pilot boat saved two men and a third swam ashore, but the survivors said a fourth man was still missing. At 11.10 the *Bassett Green* was also launched and found the outboard motor dinghy *Jaime Lewis* upside down. It transpired the four men had been in this boat, but unfortunately the search for the fourth man was unsuccessful.

Although the dinghy was not often called in 1964, it was decided, from 1965, to make Poole a regular seasonal Inshore Rescue Boat station with a full size 15½-feet craft. It was further changed to an all-the-year-round station by remaining operative throughout the winter of 1966-7. In the late summer of 1967 the second of the experimental 'Hatch' boats, designed by George Hatch, A.M.R.I.N.A., as combination fast rescue and boarding boats, was sent to Poole for evaluation trials. This boat, known as *18-03*, had crossed the English Channel to St. Malo as part of the varied flotilla of British lifeboats shown at the Tenth International Life-boat Conference held at Dinard. She is a highly sophisticated small craft 20½-feet long overall, with a Volvo Penta diesel inboard engine with outboard drive, giving 100 h.p. and capable of 24 knots in quite bad conditions.

The I.R.B. made her first rescue on the evening of July 28th 1965, when the duty officer of the Parkstone Sea Cadets reported that a dinghy with four boys was in difficulties in the harbour. A strong south-westerly wind was whipping up the shallow waters and a flood tide was running fast. The I.R.B. found that the mainstay supporting the sailing boat's mast had broken, causing the mast to fall. The boat and the four cadets were towed back to Poole.

On another occasion the shallow draught of the I.R.B. was useful. On April 16th 1967, a motor boat stranded outside the harbour entrance and a tug and pilot boat could not get near enough to help. The I.R.B. got alongside the motor boat *Two Ways* and rescued the four occupants.

In June 1969 it was decided to move *18-03* to Brixham for further trials and in the same month a 17 ft. 'Dell Quay Dory' type of rescue launch was sent to replace her at Poole. This class of lifeboat has already been described in the Lyme Regis chapter. In 1969, also, the regular lifeboat at the station, the *Bassett Green*, was withdrawn from service and replaced by a craft of similar type, the *George Elmy*, which had been at the Seaham station in county Durham. It will be seen by the service record that these new rescue craft are admirably carrying on the good work of the station.

BOAT RECORD, STUDLAND AND POOLE

Years on station	Length, Breadth, Oars/Crew	Type, Weight, Cost	Year built, (Off. no.), Builder	Boat's name, Donor, Authority
(a) at Studland				
1826- c. 1850	20' 7' 8/9	Plenty 1t5 £100	1826 Plenty, Newbury	(No name) R.N.I.P.L.S. and local subs. R.N.I.P.L.S. (Dorset Branch Association)
(a) at Poole				
1865- 1880	32' 7' 4" 10/13	SR 2t5 £210	1865 Forrestt, Limehouse	*Manley Wood*[1] An anonymous lady R.N.L.I.
1880- 1896	34' 8' 3" 10/13	SR 3t12 £363	1880 (188) Woolfe, Shadwell	*Joseph and Mary*[2] Legacy Mrs. Boetefeur, R.N.L.I. [London
1897- 1910	38' 9' 4" 12/15	W 6t13 £924	1892 (316)[3] Henderson, Glasgow	*City Masonic Club* Freemasons of the City of R.N.L.I. [London
1910- 1939	37' 6" 9' 3" 12/15	SR 5t3 £1086	1910 (608) Thames Iron Works, Blackwall	*Harmar* Legacy G. J. Harmar, R.N.L.I. [London
1939- 1962	32' 9' 3" -/7	Surf(M) 4t19 £3337	1938 (811) Groves and Guttridge, Cowes	*Thomas Kirk Wright* Legacy T. H. K. Wright, R.N.L.I. [Bournemouth
1962-9	35' 6" 10' 8" -/7	L (M) 8t3 £14038	1951 (891)[4] Groves and Guttridge, Cowes	*Bassett Green* W. H. Bassett Green, R.N.L.I. [Winchcombe
1969-	35' 6" 10' 8" -/7	L(M) 8t18 £14000	1950 (873)[5] Groves and Guttridge, Cowes	*George Elmy* Legacy Miss E. Elmy, Stoke R.N.L.I. [Newington

Inshore Rescue Boats—   1963-4   12′ rubber rowing dinghy
1964-5   12′ rubber dinghy with outboard motor
1965-   15′ 6″ standard IRB
1967-9   18′ fast rescue launch *18-03*
1969-   17′ fast rescue launch *17-003*

1 Renamed *Joseph and Mary* in 1879 on appropriation to legacy of Mrs. Boetefeur.
2 Renamed *Boy's Own No. 2* in 1882 on appropriation to fund of the *Boys' Own
Paper*
3 Built to take part in rowing trials and subsequently tried out at various stations.
4 Formerly at Padstow No. 2 station.
5 Formerly at Seaham station.

SERVICE RECORD, POOLE

Manley Wood Lifeboat
1867	Jan.	8	Brig *Antares*, of Greifswald (Germany), landed 1 and stood by	
	Nov.	16	Brig *Contest*, of Guernsey, stood by	
		17	do., landed, in three trips, 46 (10 crew and 36 labourers)	
1868	Dec.	15	Lugger *Augustine*, of Pont L'Abbé (France), saved lugger and	4
1876	Mar.	12	Ketch *William Pitt*, of Poole, saved	1
1879	Mar.	27	Ship *Martaban*, of Greenock, saved	11

Boy's Own No. 2 Lifeboat
1882	Jun.	1	Brigantine *Otto*, of Hoganas (Sweden), saved	9
1883	Jan.	9	Brig *Victor*, of Neustadt (Germany), stood by	
1891	Oct.	26	Schooner *Mountblairy*, of Plymouth, stood by	
	Nov.	11	Brig *Solertia*, of Tonsberg (Norway), saved	9
1895	Jan.	12	Barque *Brilliant*, of Grimstad (Norway), saved	10
1896	Feb.	23	Brigantine *Albert T. Young*, of Faversham, landed 6	
			do. (second launch), stood by	

Reserve Lifeboat
1897	Jan.	23	Steam launch Zulu, of Poole, landed 2

City Masonic Club Lifeboat
1898	Nov,	23	Schooner *Velocity*, of Leith, assisted Swanage lifeboat bringing rescued crew to Poole	
		24	Three-masted schooner *Frier*, of Porsgrunn (Norway), saved	8

William Erle Lifeboat (of Swanage, with a Poole crew)
Barque *Bonne Mère*, of Havre, gave help and stood by
do. (second launch), stood by

City Masonic Club Lifeboat
			Barque *Bonne Mère*, of Havre, stood by	
		25	do., assisted to save vessel (taken to Southampton) and	13
1900	Dec.	24	Steamship *Matin*, of Sunderland, stood by	
1902	Feb.	5	Ketch *Little Jessie*, of Grimsby, stood by	
1904	Dec.	4	Schooner *Carrie Bell*, of Lancaster, stood by	
			Ketch *Zenobia*, of London, assisted to save vessel	
1908	Oct.	21	Ketch *Conquest*, of Bridgwater, saved	5
1910	Jan.	11	Fourteen fishing boats, of Poole, stood by at harbour entrance	

Harmar Lifeboat
1913	Dec.	19	Barge *Emma and John*, of London, saved	2
			do. (second launch), saved barge	
1914	Nov.	21	Ketch *Lord Alcester*, of London, landed 4	

1914	Dec.	28	Fishing boat *Eclipse*, of Poole, saved boat and	2
1915	Nov.	13	H.M. Steam trawler *King Heron*, saved	10
1916	Oct.	22	H.M. Steam drifter *Fame*, saved	7
1917	Mar.	3	Ketch *Boaz*, of Ipswich, assisted to save ketch	
1919	Jan.	8	Ex-German submarine *U.143*, stood by	
			Schooner *Zwaluw*, of Antwerp, saved	9
		9	Ex-German submarine *U.143*, saved	28
1921	Apr.	21-22	Steamship *Fernande*, of Ostend (Belgium), stood by	
1922	Oct.	15	Schooner *Sidney*, of Guernsey, stood by	
		29	Motor vessel *Pioneer*, of Guernsey, stood by and gave help	
1926	Feb.	17	Fishing boats, of Poole, stood by	
1931	Feb.	18	Barge *Genesta*, of Cowes, gave help	
1932	Mar.	28	Yacht *Capri*, of Fleetwood, towed yacht and 6 to safety	
	Nov.	13	Steamship *Pitwines*, of London, stood by and assisted to refloat	
1933	Dec.	5	Yawl yacht *Glencora*, of Falmouth, saved	2
1935	Sep.	28	Converted ship's boat, stood by and towed into harbour	
1938	Jun.	1	Motor yacht *Zaire*, of Poole, landed 1	

Thomas Kirk Wright Lifeboat

1939	Jan.	22	Motor launch *Snapper*, of Poole, towed in launch and 1	
1940	Jan.	1	Motor cruiser *Sea Mist*, of Poole, saved yacht and	3
1946	Apr.	21	Motor boat *Skylark*, of Poole, saved	1
	Jul.	14	Fishing boat *SV. 107*,of Christchurch, saved drifting boat	
1947	Sep.	17	'Spitfire' aeroplane, salved wreckage	
1949	Sep.	4	Motor yacht *Audrey*, of Poole, landed 1	
1953	Oct.	7	Yacht *Freda*, of Hamble, saved yacht and	4
1954	Aug.	7	Cabin cruiser *Elsie*, of Wareham, towed home yacht and 4	
	Sep.	24	Yacht *Mouette N.*, of Poole, saved yacht	
1955	Mar.	26	Motor launch *Renif*, of Poole, towed home launch and 2	
1956	Apr.	30	Sailing dinghy, saved dinghy and landed 2	
1957	Mar.	11	Motor boat, saved boat and	3
	May	29	Yacht *Brief Encounter*, of Southampton, saved yacht and	2
	Jul.	7	Dinghy, landed 3 and the dinghy	
	Sep.	27	Cabin cruiser *Rani IV*, of London, towed in boat and 4	
	Nov.	30	Motor vessel *Dollard*, of Rotterdam, stood by	
1958	Aug.	4	Cabin cruiser *Chloe*, of Southampton, landed 5	
	Sep.	27	Yacht *Yarinya*, of Poole, refloated yacht (6 on board) and moored safely	
			Auxiliary yacht *Cossar*, refloated and remoored yacht, landed 4	
1959	Jan.	2	Sailing dinghy *Stormwind*, saved dinghy and	1
	Dec.	6	Motor boat *Sandbanks Queen*, gave help	
1960	Jul.	17	Yacht *Forella*, of London, landed 2	
1961	Feb.	5	Small motor cruiser, saved boat and	1
	Jul.	21	Motor launch, escorted launch and 2 to safe berth	

Bassett Green Lifeboat

1962	Aug.	14	Yacht *Cashlow*, escorted yacht and 2 to safe anchorage	
	Sep.	29	Yacht *Margara Della*, saved	2
		30	Cabin cruiser *Sea Knight*, saved vessel	
1963	Aug.	28	Cabin cruiser *Sarnia*, saved vessel and landed 6	
	Sep.	1	Cabin cruiser *Seabreeze*, landed 3	
1964	May	1	Outboard motor dinghy *Jaime Lewis*, saved dinghy	
1965	Apr.	24	Yacht *Cygnet*, towed yacht to harbour	
1966	Mar.	27	Motor launch, saved launch and	3
1968	Nov.	17	Cutter yacht *Wind*, saved yacht and	2
1969	Apr.	6	Trimaran *Karina Two*, towed in yacht and 2	

George Elmy Lifeboat

1969	Nov.	3	Yacht *Tilaer*, saved boat and	2
	Dec.	6	Training ship *Ruhr*, landed a sick man, saving his life	1
		21	Fishing boat *Frome Lady*, of Poole, towed in boat and 7	

Inshore Rescue Boat

1965	Jul.	28	Sailing dinghy, saved dinghy and	4
	Aug.	4	Sailing craft *Ajax*, gave help	
	Sep.	30	Small boat, landed 1	
1967	Mar.	5	Motor boat *Duck*, saved boat	
	Apr.	5	Canoe, gave help	
		16	Motor boat *Two Ways*, saved	4
	May	22	Cabin cruiser, saved vessel and	1
	Dec.	9	Cabin cruiser *Chilten Dean*, gave help and landed 2	
1968	Apr.	11	Speed boat, escorted boat	
	Sep.	1	Motor boat *Skewer*, landed 2	
	Dec.	28	Yacht *Trewent II*, gave help	
1969	Apr.	6	Cabin cruiser *Gay Lady*, escorted boat	

Rescue launch *18-03*

1967	Sep.	5	Yacht *Calypso V*, landed 3
1968	Apr.	10	Cabin cruiser *Menewethan*, gave help
	July	10	Missing person, landed 1
	Sep.	1	Sailing boat, landed 2
			Cabin cruiser *Maimie Rob*, gave help and landed 8

Rescue launch *17-003*

1969	June	25	Speedboat, saved boat and	3
	Oct.	10	Sailing yacht *Barbizon*, saved yacht and	1

The WRECK AND RESCUE Series [General Editor: Grahame Farr] are standard histories of Britain's lifeboats, recording the story of each station from its inception to the present day, complete with Boat and Service Records. They also detail innumerable stories of shipwrecks round this island's shores, and include many historic photographs of these wrecks. An index volume, plus a general introductory volume to the Series, are also planned.

WRECK AND RESCUE ROUND THE CORNISH COAST
Cyril Noall and Grahame Farr

I. THE STORY OF THE NORTH COAST LIFEBOATS
Bude — Port Isaac — Padstow — Newquay — Hayle
126 pages . 14 plates . maps

II. THE STORY OF THE LAND'S END LIFEBOATS
St. Ives — Sennen — Isles of Scilly — Penzance — Newlyn — Penlee
Porthleven
151 pages . 29 plates . maps

III. THE STORY OF THE SOUTH COAST LIFEBOATS
Mullion — The Lizard — Cadgwith — Coverack — Porthoustock — Falmouth — Portloe — Mevagissey — Polkerris — Fowey — Looe
195 pages . 29 plates . maps

WRECK AND RESCUE IN THE BRISTOL CHANNEL
Grahame Farr

I. THE STORY OF THE ENGLISH LIFEBOATS
   Clovelly — Appledore — Northam Burrows — Braunton Burrows — Morte Bay — Ilfracombe — Lynmouth — Minehead — Watchet — Burnham — Weston-super-Mare
   183 pages . 26 plates . maps

II. THE STORY OF THE WELSH LIFEBOATS
   Penarth — Barry Dock — Atlantic College — Porthcawl — Port Talbot — Swansea — The Mumbles — Port Eynon — Llanelli — Burry Port — Pembrey — Ferryside — Tenby — Angle
   190 pages . 28 plates . maps

WRECK AND RESCUE ON THE ESSEX COAST
Robert Malster

THE STORY OF ESSEX LIFEBOATS
Harwich — Walton — Frinton — Clacton — Southend-on-Sea — the salvaging smacks — the lifeboat builders of Essex
168 pages . 20 plates . map

WRECK AND RESCUE ON THE COAST OF DEVON
Grahame Farr

THE STORY OF THE SOUTH DEVON LIFEBOATS
Plymouth — Yealm River — Hope Cove — Salcombe — Dartmouth — Brixham/Torbay — Torquay — Teignmouth — Exmouth — Sidmouth
196 pages . 37 plates . maps

WRECK AND RESCUE ON THE COAST OF WALES
Henry Parry

I. THE LIFEBOATS OF CARDIGAN BAY AND ANGLESEY
   Barmouth — Criccieth/Portmadoc — Pwllheli — Abersoch — Porthdinllaen — Llanaelhaiarn — Llanddwyn — Rhosneigr — Rhoscolyn — Holyhead
   148 pages . 20 plates . maps

II. THE STORY OF THE NORTH WALES LIFEBOATS
   Cemlyn — Cemaes — Bull Bay — Moelfre — Penmon — Beaumaris — Llandudno — Llandulas — Abergele — Rhyl — Point of Ayr — Mostyn